Advance Pra
Work Less, I

CW00666456

"There are two things I hear over and over again from agency owners: 1) I'm making less than I would if I went to work for someone again; and 2) I'm working more than I would if I were working for someone again. There is no reason you should work more or earn less when running your own business, which is why you must read this book. Karl Sakas breaks down a doable process that allows you to gain control of your life—and your business."

–**Gini Dietrich**, founder and author of *Spin Sucks*

"A creative agency has two stages of success: the initial success derived from hard work, and the more lucrative level of success that is untethered from effort. In *Work Less, Earn More*, Karl gives you a framework to finally get to the elusive second level."

–**Blair Enns**, founder of Win Without Pitching and author of *Pricing Creativity: A Guide to Profit Beyond the Billable Hour*

"When I think of advisors who take their craft seriously, listen carefully, and formulate practical and actionable concepts, Karl is a master at that, and this tome is a great example of that expertise."

–**David C. Baker**, advisory lead at Punctuation and author of *Expertise* and *Tradecraft*

"I desperately wish this essential guide had been published a decade ago, as it would have saved me a lot of hassles and heartache! This is an absolutely essential guide for every agency owner."

–**Jay Baer**, marketing and CX strategist and co-author of *Talk Triggers*

"I can say, emphatically and from firsthand experience, that Karl is the real deal. He understands the pain points that agency owners face every day, and he anticipates the pitfalls down that road that most owners haven't even thought of yet. *Work Less, Earn More* is a crucial tool for anyone who wants to make the most of the opportunities that agency ownership presents."

—**Chris Dreyer**, CEO and owner of Rankings.io

"*Work Less, Earn More* is the right book at the right time for so many agency owners out there. Too many of us sacrifice our days (and nights) to deadlines, last-minute team requests, or client fires. Karl brings his brilliant mind (and big heart) to our industry with this must-read book. If you're an agency owner seeking meaning, boundaries, and more income, this better be the next book you read."

—**Brent Weaver**, CEO and founder of UGURUS

"Being an agency owner often feels like a lonely—and thankless—job. *Work Less, Earn More* is your step-by-step guide to leading the agency (and life!) you want, and on your terms."

—**Tamsen Webster,** message strategist

"Karl is on the money again. His advice and experience once again resonate for anyone looking to 'Build a Better Agency' and dare I say 'Life'. Thank you Karl for bringing so much together in one place."

—**Steve Krull**, CEO of Be Found Online

"*Work Less, Earn More* belongs on the bookshelf of every creative leader or CEO. It is timely, insightful, and actionable, just like Karl Sakas. For any owner that wants to level up their company and team, this book is for you."

—**Cathy Atkins,** owner of Metis Communications

"Karl is an agency whisperer. As my agency coach, Karl helped me to manage my agency more effectively, and he guided me through countless client emergencies with his thoughtful frameworks and communications tools. This book distills all the lessons I learned from years of working directly with Karl into one succinct guide. Reading this book will help you lead a more profitable, well-run agency, but more importantly it will save you from losing sleep over client and staff emergencies. Reading this book is an investment in your well-being as an agency owner, and it's well worth your time."

—**Erin Bury**, CEO of Willful

"Working less while making more may sound like a false promise to many agency owners. But the truth is... I've seen hundreds of agency owners do it! Karl's [*Work Less, Earn More*] book is packed with practical tips and hacks for doing just that. I dare you to read it and not put some of his counsel into action."

—**Drew McLellan**, CEO/Partner of the
Agency Management Institute

"This valuable book is like a personal GPS for every agency owner. Pay careful attention to Karl's brilliant strategies, valuable frameworks, and practical advice to focus on the best direction to design your journey, grow your team, and build revenue for your agency."

—**Neen James**, executive strategist

"Intentionality drives results for the very best agency teams I've worked with. In *Work Less, Earn More*, Karl Sakas gifts you with a clear, concise roadmap to intentionally creating the agency you desire and the life you love."

—**Gray MacKenzie**, co-founder of ZenPilot

"Karl has the ability to help agency owners see their own opportunities more clearly, and his methodologies are easy to implement, but game-changing. This book is a must-read if you're feeling burned out from the grind of agency ownership."

–**Tara Coomans**, CEO of Avaans Media

For more, visit WorkLessEarnMoreBook.com

Work Less, Earn More

How to Escape the Daily Grind of Agency Ownership

Karl Sakas

Sakas & Company

Foreword by Carl Smith of the Bureau of Digital

First Edition

Ready to accelerate your progress?

Get free companion tools at **WorkLessEarnMoreBook.com**

Please send your questions, comments, and feedback (even the typos!) to Concierge@SakasAndCompany.com

(FAQ: **It's pronounced "say-kiss."**)

Copyright © 2023 by Karl A. Sakas
All rights reserved.
All external content is the property of its respective owner(s).

First Edition

ISBN: 979-8-9871445-0-3   Hardcover
        979-8-9871445-2-7   Paperback
        979-8-9871445-3-4   eBook
        979-8-9871445-4-1   Audiobook

Obligatory Disclaimer:

Applying this advice will likely help you, but your mileage may vary.

What's an "agency"? A firm that provides marketing, design, development, strategy, or related professional services on a for-hire basis for other organizations. (And yes, that includes even the "we're-not-an-agency" agencies.)

I'm not an accountant, lawyer, financial planner, or medical expert. Be sure to get custom-to-you advice from the appropriate professional.

For simplicity's sake, I'll primarily refer to financial numbers in U.S. dollars, as of the book's publication. A majority of the examples are U.S.-centric. But most concepts will *likely* apply regardless of where you live and work. After all, if you run an agency—you want to do work you're proud of, with clients and team members you like, while getting paid a reasonable (or maybe more-than-reasonable) amount.

~~Work~~ Less, Earn More

How to Escape the Daily Grind of Agency Ownership
By Karl Sakas. Foreword by Carl Smith

Foreword

If you're reading this, you're either running a digital shop or you're thinking about it. If that's the case, then don't put this book down! It has everything you need to get to the next level, no matter your current level.

Karl has guided hundreds of agency founders down the path to becoming an actual owner vs. being an employee in their own company. And he's willing to show all of us the way. What's amazing is he does this regardless of where we are in our entrepreneurial journey. Are you an established shop facing financial challenges? Just starting out and not enough time to get everything done? Facing a personal crisis but not able to walk away or everything will fall apart? He's seen it all and has helped other owners through it.

Perhaps the most valuable part of the book is the exercises. I know, I know. I always want to skip past them, too. But with what Karl has created, you can actually see the progress as you complete each one. Personally, understanding what owner stage I'm in was the most eye-opening. And while I've been stuck in the same spot for a while, I now know why and have the playbook to evolve into the type of owner I want to be and my company wants me to be.

There's just one thing I don't understand. Why the heck he would put it all in writing? And make it so easy to find the solutions we need? The guy is gonna write himself out of a job!

–**Carl Smith**, owner, Bureau of Digital

Dedication

This book is dedicated to YOU, as the owner (or future owner) of a marketing agency, design studio, digital shop, or other creative firm.

As an independent agency owner, you want to create a better life for yourself and your family—with help from everyone supporting you on that journey.

Running an agency will never be "easy"—but it doesn't have to be so hard. I hope this book helps you reach your goals faster, more smoothly, and more profitably than if you were working on your own.

Thanks to the hundreds of agency owners I've worked with directly and the thousands more who've been inspired to change their agency for the better.

–**Karl Sakas**, founder, Sakas & Company

Preface

There is, I believe, something uniquely complicated about agencies as a business. And this unfortunate uniqueness means we need a book like *Work Less, Earn More*.

Yes, something like precision manufacturing is more complicated on an *absolute* basis. But building jet engines or providing life-or-death healthcare services is—for those businesses—typically a profitable, billion-dollar opportunity.

In contrast, agencies have the highly complicated situation of matching humans on both sides of the equation: team members inside the business and clients outside the business. But they're typically producing just seven or eight figures in revenue, and only six or seven figures of annual earnings. That isn't peanuts, but it often doesn't cover the "stress penalty."

Compared to other service businesses, clients of agencies tend to have particular expectations about the mostly intangible work that agencies do. When a CMO hires a plumber to deal with a problem at their house, it's not too hard to determine if the plumber did a good job: Things work again, or they don't. But when that same CMO hires an agency, now they have all kinds of opinions about what "good" looks like.

Yes, there are other service businesses that rely on expertise that may not be fully validated until after the last check clears (a so-called "credence good"). For instance, you trust that your CPA or your lawyer has given you good advice. But there's an important difference: despite all the lawyer and accountant jokes, people tend to pay invoices from their CPA and their business attorney promptly.

In contrast? As an agency operations manager, I once sent a prepaid FedEx label to a squirrelly client because their accounting department couldn't seem to find time to mail us a past-due check.

Most clients wouldn't ask their lawyer for a price cut or question their accountant's expertise. Yet those same clients are quick to demand a price cut—or free work—from their agency because those clients don't fully respect the work. *To be fair,* some *agencies have earned that lack of respect.*

On top of this, many agency leaders are what I'd call "accidental" agency owners. They fell into running the business due to their expertise and passion for the work, without any prior business training. Sometimes, they don't have prior experience even working as an employee at an agency. (This is true for at least one-third of my clients.)

Combine those three factors (a complex business with humans on all sides, subjectively picky clients who don't fully respect the agency's expertise, and a business typically led by a craftsperson-turned-CEO), and agencies are often a recipe for disaster.

Even worse? For most agency owners, the business is their #1 or #2 financial asset. Their family is *counting on them* to succeed.

I love working with agencies so much that it's been my *only* focus for over a decade. Agency owners are smart, creative, interesting people. But they're playing against a stacked deck.

Fortunately, you *can* reclaim that work/life balance—and *Work Less, Earn More* gives you a step-by-step roadmap to make it happen.

Let's go!

Get Free Resources

As the owner of this book, you have free access to templates and other digital resources to help you accelerate your *Work Less, Earn More* journey—all available at no charge via the companion workbook.

This includes a place to track your answers to the exercises in the book, along with electronic versions of tools you'll see in the book.

At more than 30 pages in length, the companion workbook is based on the curriculum from my annual "Work Less, Earn More" bootcamp program... but you're getting access for the price of this book.

Ready to jumpstart your progress? To get instant opt-in access to all the time-saving resources, visit **WorkLessEarnMoreBook.com**

Table of Contents

Foreword, Dedication, Preface, and Free Resources

Introduction: **Escaping the Daily Grind**   1

Chapter 1: **Design Your Ideal Agency**   15

Chapter 2: **Four Stages of Day-to-Day Involvement**   27

Chapter 3: **Grow Your Support Team**   45

Chapter 4: **Work Less**   65

Chapter 5: **Earn More**   81

Chapter 6: **Enlist Your Team**   97

Chapter 7: **Strategies and Tactics to Grow**   115

Chapter 8: **Choose Your Growth Strategy**   131

Chapter 9: **Create Your Custom 90-Day Plan**   139

Chapter 10: **Hold Yourself Accountable**   151

Chapter 11: **Take Action**   159

Additional Reading   165

Acknowledgements   168

About the Author   171

Introduction:

Escaping the Daily Grind of Agency Ownership

Get to Your Ideal Future

As an agency owner, you want to get paid what you deserve—to increase your take-home pay, to grow your business, to fund passion projects, to secure your family's financial future.

You likely don't dream of working *more* hours, or *more* nights and weekends. Yet many agency owners feel they're constantly in the weeds, working *in* their business rather than *on* their business—instead of getting to spend that time with their loved ones or on other things they care about. They feel like they need more hours in the day to get it all done.

If working less and/or earning more sounds appealing, go ahead and imagine your ideal future: You're doing work you enjoy, with people you like, on the schedule you want, with the compensation you deserve. Your stress levels are a *lot* lower. And you're feeling more confident about your business—and about life in general, including how you'll actually make all of this happen.

Fortunately, the extra time and money are *already* within your reach— and there's a step-by-step process you can use to make it happen.

That's the purpose behind "Work Less, Earn More," a virtual bootcamp for agency owners that I've distilled into this book. Of course, a book isn't a replacement for group coaching or one-on-one consulting, but by investing your time reading this and filling out the companion workbook, you'll be able to learn and implement the adaptive process that gets you closer to your ideal future.

There is no one "right" way for every agency owner to reach their goals (hence this iterative, adaptive process), but there are certain benchmarks and practices that can get you there. Applying this advice will likely help you, but your mileage may vary. Every agency is unique and may require additional support.

This Book Is for You

If the ideal future above is what you're working toward (or *want* to work toward), this book is for you.

More specifically, this book is for owners of marketing and creative agencies—companies delivering mostly-intangible services whose quality depends highly on the team's expertise and delivery. You might call your business a digital agency, a creative studio, a development shop, a PR firm, a video production house, or something else.

The bottom line is this: If your company does creative or marketing work for paying clients, congratulations! **You're an agency owner, which means this book can help you Work Less and Earn More.**

What Does It Really Mean to "Work Less"?

While "work less" might seem too obvious a term to define, the reality is that working less will look different for each person.

For instance, that *could* look like working fewer than 40 hours a week. Or it might involve going from 80-hour weeks to 60-hour weeks. And some want to eliminate their agency role entirely to move on to something new.

Sometimes, working less is about *higher-quality* hours. For instance, you might dislike sales... yet serve as the primary salesperson. Or perhaps you're doing client billables when you'd rather focus on things like long-term vision, culture, and partnership-building. In this case, it's about shifting the *content* of the work, rather than reducing the hours.

For others, it might not be about *either* of those—maybe you just want to stop thinking about work all. the. time.

Once you identify your ideal outcome, you can follow the *Work Less, Earn More* process to get there. You'll create and implement a strategy that gets you to that ideal work life—whether it's spending fewer hours in the office and more with your family, getting to focus on the work you love, or being able to keep work at work, so you can finally enjoy some well-deserved time off.

Importantly, *you* get to choose what this looks like for you. Let's take some time to clarify your personal definition of "work less."

OPTIONAL EXERCISE: Based on where you are today, what does "work less" look like for you? Share your answer here—or complete the prompt in the companion workbook. Download your copy at WorkLessEarnMoreBook.com.

Being a Workaholic: What If You Don't Want to Work Less?

Do you *have* to work less? Not necessarily; it's up to you.

If you identify as a workaholic and it's not a problem for you (and those around you), you're welcome to skip changing things. But if your being a workaholic has become a problem, consider seeking professional support from a therapist or other advisor; this has been helpful in my own life.

Some agency owners I've worked with have mentioned they've gotten bored after delegating their workload to their team. Some may choose to get more involved again, while others may use that as the springboard to pursue a new direction in life. Either way, it's nice to have options.

And if you love the work you're doing now...

Not sure if you need to change anything about the way you work right now? That's okay!

This book can help you optimize *where* you spend your time. That way, you'll get the most from the hours you work... which ultimately helps you earn more. Speaking of that...

What Does It Really Mean to "Earn More"?

Earning "more" is also relative. Generally, owners will make a six-figure salary plus shareholder distributions from a portion of their 20-30% net profit margins. Multi-owner agencies tend to pay each owner less (per person) than single-owner agencies.

Some agency owners are happy at $150,000 a year. Others are unhappy at $500,000 and want to hit $1 million or more. (Note that very few independent agency owners are taking a $1 million salary, although plenty have overall income exceeding $1 million after you include pass-through profits.)

While $500,000 (or more) may seem high to some—including your employees—earning more for the sake of earning more isn't the end goal. Your business enables your family's personal financial goals. You might be saving for retirement and college tuition, buying your dream home (or a second home), and traveling to once-in-a-lifetime destinations. For many, a healthy income meets their goals—while others want the bigger potential payday of a big exit.

What If You Don't Want to Earn More?

If you're currently making less than six figures, consider whether you're being adequately compensated for the risk of running a business. As I share in the "Earn More" chapter, consider reading the book *Overcoming Underearning*.

If your salary is at the lower end of six figures, but you're happy with your standard of living—consider what earning more might mean for you.

Would earning more create new possibilities and help you reach your goals faster? Would it help you retire early? Send your kids to a more expensive college? Upgrade your current lifestyle? What would become *easier* if you earned more?

OPTIONAL EXERCISE: Based on where you are today, what does "earn more" look like for you? Fill out the prompt here—or in the companion workbook.

What's Your Growth Style?

Before you can start working less and earning more, you need to determine your *why*. There are several whys to outline in this process; more on that in the next chapter. But to start, dig into why you want to grow your agency. This is what I call your agency's **"Growth Style"**:

◊ In a **Lifestyle**-oriented agency, your goal is to run a profitable business to fund a comfortable lifestyle. You're still *growing*, but likely growing less than 30% a year. This is the default for the agency business model.

◊ In an **Equity**-oriented agency, also known as a "high-growth" business, your goal is to sell the agency. Outside of the agency world, this typically revolves around making highly scalable products. But it's doable in the agency business model if you make the right decisions (and execute well) along the way.

Knowing this from the get-go will help you make better decisions throughout the *Work Less, Earn More* process. Why? Because happy agency owners typically make business choices that are consistent with their agency growth style on the Lifestyle vs. Equity continuum.

Neither is better than the other, and most agency owners fall somewhere in the middle of the spectrum. But knowing your values helps you optimize your agency's model for sustainable growth. And that means more time and money for you, as the business owner.

OPTIONAL EXERCISE: Fill out the Lifestyle vs. Equity quiz in the companion workbook.

What's Your Growth Personality Type?

Your preferred "**Growth Personality Type**" impacts your agency's growth, recruiting, profits, and quality of life. To generalize, there are two types of growth personalities:

◊ **Maximizers** tend to prioritize **raw returns**, or getting maximum revenues and profits.

◊ **Optimizers** prioritize **ROI**, or seeking results *relative* to the investment required.

Maximization is exciting—it's about rapid growth that makes you feel like you're running a tech startup. (Note: your agency is *not* a tech startup. If you operate like it is, you're in for some very high highs... and very low lows.)

In contrast, optimization is about balancing effectiveness and efficiency. You're still growing, but you're prioritizing sustainability over big, flashy numbers. Optimization is a long-term strategy.

Here are some ways to tell whether you're a Maximizer vs. Optimizer.

You might be a Maximizer if:

◊ You want to grow revenue more than 2X in the coming year (for instance, you want to 3X or 4X your revenue in 12 months).

◊ You and your team regularly work 80+ hours a week.

◊ Employee turnover is significantly higher than 20% annually.

◊ You believe more clients = more money.

◊ You believe that if you jump, the net will always appear—especially when it comes to finding work for the people to hire.

You might be an Optimizer if:

◊ You don't automatically say "yes" when a client or employee requests something.

◊ You've set revenue goals for the year, including baseline and reach goals, as well as a revenue plan.

◊ Your goal is to get maximum client results, as long as they are within the context of their budget and what you can accomplish via white-hat marketing techniques.

◊ You're typically working less than 45 hours a week.

◊ You work with an advisor to get feedback on where to optimize and how to improve.

As with growth styles, neither is inherently better than the other, and agency owners often fall somewhere in the middle of the spectrum. However, as you might imagine from the *Work Less, Earn More* model, my approach is more about optimization rather than maximization.

Optimizers are realistic about their potential. They're still often growing rapidly—for instance, seeking to double their revenue in 1-3 years—but they execute according to a plan. Optimizers don't rely on happy accidents.

While Maximizers' optimism is inspiring, they're often unable to break away from short-term firefighting to focus on long-term goals, no matter how their employees and their advisors try to help. This distractedness tends to hurt their client and employee retention, and it becomes a vicious cycle.

What if you're a committed Maximizer? You'll benefit from the "earn more" portions of this book. But I'd encourage you to stay open-minded about *how* you approach growth, or else you're likely to burn out early.

OPTIONAL EXERCISE: Fill out the Growth Personality Type quiz in the companion workbook.

Finding Meaning in Your Work

As a business owner, you're in a privileged position. You get to create your day-to-day reality. This includes choosing (to at least *some* extent) your employees, clients, and partners. You set the direction of the business. If there are problems, that means you're responsible for fixing them... but that also means you have the power to do so.

When things are running smoothly, you're paid well for carrying these responsibilities. And if you're *not* paid well, you can fix that.

Yet once you're paid well, you've created a new problem. When you're doing well financially and can do almost anything you want with your time, you might start experiencing ennui—a sense of listlessness and lack of purpose. For instance, a dentist client years ago had one Porsche... but they wished they had a *second* Porsche, like their competitor down the street. Yet would that second Porsche make their life appreciably better?

Thus, you face a new challenge: **is your work giving you the *meaning* you want?**

Some agency owners fall into the trap of believing that their team is responsible for giving them meaning, by the team *appreciating* the owner. After all, you're working hard for them!

To be blunt, that's not their job. **Your team is not responsible for appreciating you**. They are being paid to do a job. But as the business owner, it *is* your responsibility to create a healthy environment that promotes individual growth and relative autonomy over one's work— which will ultimately lead to a better work quality and sustainable growth for the business.

Once you're ready to separate your self-worth from how others feel about you, it's time to **find what *really* brings meaning to your life**.

Everyone has their own definition of what's meaningful. But agency owners typically find meaning in one or more of these areas:

◊ The **industries** you serve (e.g., focusing on non-profits or other mission-based organizations, serving faith-based organizations, or doing marketing for sustainability-oriented businesses);

◊ The **clients** you serve (e.g., helping small business owners create a better life for themselves and their families);

◊ The **resources** you commit to worthy causes (e.g., "1% for the Planet," *pro bono* work, or company-based philanthropy);

◊ The **work environment** you create for your team (e.g., creating a well-run business where employees and contractors feel valued financially and otherwise and have opportunities to reach their goals);

◊ The **sum of the parts** (e.g., pursuing a never-ending passion for optimizing the agency as a business); or

◊ Your **non-work life** (e.g., focusing on family, friends, or projects outside of the agency... which creates an incentive to work less).

Which of those seem like a match for you? Finding happiness and meaning in your life is ultimately beyond the scope of this book. You may want to talk with a therapist, spiritual advisor, or other confidant(e) to help you work through these. It might be tempting to put this off... but that can eventually turn into a full-blown existential crisis.

Knowing that you're ultimately responsible for finding your own meaning means you'll be more focused on building the ideal agency for *you*. And that's better for everyone, in the long run.

I hope this section helps point you in your own right direction as you create a more meaningful-to-you life.

OPTIONAL EXERCISE: Based on where you are today, what's your primary motivation as you seek meaning (from the preceding list, or otherwise)? Share here, or fill out the prompt in the companion workbook.

What's Next?

I know this is a lot to take in—congrats on making it here! You're ready to take the next step, to begin building a custom roadmap to reach your goals.

In the next chapter, I'll share a framework to help you start organizing and outlining *your* ideal version of work less, earn more, so you can start turning that into reality.

This step-by-step framework has already helped leaders at agencies worldwide. The framework? You're going to **design your ideal agency**!

TL; DR*
Introduction: Escaping the Daily Grind of Agency Ownership

In a hurry? Here's what to know:

♦ Aimed at owners of marketing and creative agencies, *Work Less, Earn More* is a step-by-step process to help you improve your work/life balance.

♦ That is: you can do work you enjoy, with people you like, on the schedule you want, with the compensation you deserve.

♦ "Work less" and "earn more" are relative terms; you get to choose. Working less might mean fewer hours or a shift to higher-quality hours. And earning more might mean getting to seven figures or a healthy increase within six figures.

♦ Start by understanding how you choose to operate—including whether you're running a Lifestyle or Equity business, and whether you're a Maximizer or an Optimizer.

♦ As you move forward, you may find yourself looking for a deeper sense of meaning in your work.

♦ These foundations will prepare you for success as you build your "Work Less, Earn More" plan. But now, on to designing your ideal agency!

* "TL;DR" is shorthand for "too long; didn't read." I've included a section like this at the end of each chapter, to help if you prefer to skim the book first.

Chapter 1:

Design Your Ideal Agency

Become Clear About What Success Looks Like for You

Are you ready to work less and earn more, starting today? Great! This book will guide you through the steps to get there.

But you can't start building your ideal agency without being clear about what success looks like for you—meaning your first step should be a (brief) pause for personal reflection.

Where Do You Want to Go?

Specifically, consider these three key questions:

1. Why did you start (or join) your agency?

2. How have those expectations matched up to reality?

3. What will it take to bridge the gap to your ideal future?

The answers to those questions will serve as the foundation of your roadmap to success—milestones that clarify where you are now and where you're going. They will also give you a better understanding of what needs to change so you can get there, including where you'll enlist your team to help.

Consider agency CEO **Rhoan Morgan**. She founded her technology-focused marketing consultancy, **DemandLab**, because of her passion for marketing technology and a love of serving clients. Eight years later, the agency was doing well—with marquee clients, a hybrid team, and recognition as a trusted advisor to CMOs. But Rhoan knew she could do more.

She reached out to me for help. Together we worked on an agency roadmap process, doing a deep dive into how the agency operated and what we could do to align the company with Rhoan's vision. Ultimately, we identified two initial goals:

1. Refining and organizing the agency's delivery process to maximize client satisfaction by getting their house in order.

2. Ensuring that her agency's team culture was top-notch and that her employees were as happy and satisfied as her clients.

Based on this roadmap, I was able to create a growth strategy and a step-by-step implementation plan for DemandLab, customizing my advice to fit the agency's culture.

By empowering employees as leaders and streamlining systems and processes, the agency's executive team now had more time to focus on strategic initiatives, laying the groundwork for record growth.

Over four years, DemandLab grew revenue 52%—and quadrupled revenue-per-client. After identifying key shifts to the company's internal structure, they were able to go fully remote in 2018. The fully distributed global team continues to grow and thrive because of the early strategic planning and systems that were put in place.

Her team is empowered and happy in their work, and Rhoan is able to work a normal schedule, reclaiming nights and weekends. By envisioning what she wanted at the beginning of the process, we could create a plan to reach—and exceed—her goals

What if you have business partners?

What if you have a business partner (or partners) and you're not on the same page about what you each want?

Encourage them to do the exercises in this book, and then compare your answers... and adjust expectations accordingly.

You may find you're more aligned than you realize. And if you're not, you can decide whether your ideal future happens with or without each other.

Exercise: Your Original Vision vs. Reality

Let's reflect on the first two key questions with a brief exercise. *If you're tempted to skip the exercises, be aware that it will likely slow your long-term progress toward working less and earning more.*

EXERCISE: Reflect on the following questions. Record your answers here, in a doc on your computer or phone, or in the corresponding page of the companion workbook. Download your copy at WorkLessEarnMoreBook.com.

Why did you start (or join) your agency?

How has that matched up to reality? To what extent is the business meeting your current wants and needs?

Write an Advance Retrospective

Now that you've pinpointed where you *currently* are, it's time to determine how to begin your journey.

Start by visualizing your ideal destination. Steven Covey popularized "begin with the end in mind" in his best-selling book *The 7 Habits of Highly Effective People*, and this strategy works regardless of where you are today.

The concept urges you to think about the future—where do you *want* to find yourself? What does *your* ideal look like?

It's very personal: **What does success mean to *you*?**

Premise: You're looking backward from a hypothetical future, as if it has already happened

There's a powerful tool I use to coach agency owners. I call it the **"Advance Retrospective."** This tool helps you get unstuck by understanding what ideal future you want.

The tool guides your efforts, and you can refer to it in the future when you need motivation. I've created ones for myself annually since 2010, when I was an agency's director of client services.

In an Advance Retrospective, you'll write about your ideal future as if it's the present. You'll talk about what your day looks like and the people with whom you interact. You can also write about how you *feel* in the future, compared to how you feel today.

Don't shortchange yourself by skipping this step—clear goals lead to a clear plan of action, to help you work less and earn more.

Benefits of an Advance Retrospective

Here's how the Advance Retrospective tool will help you:

◊ It fills in the gaps between where you are now and where you want to be.

◊ It outlines what's important to you in getting there.

◊ It can guide day-to-day decisions at your agency (e.g., "Will this choice help me get to my ideal future?").

◊ Scheduling time for this exercise lets you step away from putting out daily fires so you can focus on working on your agency.

◊ Sharing this with your team will give them clarity about your vision—and help them help you reach that vision faster.

Getting started: Think about five years from now

An advance retrospective can be written from the perspective of any amount of time from now—one day away, ten years away, or on a milestone future date.

For the purposes of this *Work Less, Earn More* exercise, you'll **choose a date five years from now**. Why five years? It's long enough to have put your plan into action and start seeing results... without feeling "forever" away.

Consider including these topics

It's normal to feel overwhelmed when you're thinking about the future, so don't worry if you're not sure how to get started. Here are some questions to consider:

◊ What does your daily agenda look like?

◊ Which people are you working with closely? Who's involved in different aspects of your day? What are they like and how do you feel working with them?

◊ What kind of decisions are you making?

◊ How much time are you dedicating to working *in* the agency vs. *on* the agency?

◊ What does your work/life balance look like?

◊ How are your stress levels? How is your general quality of life?

◊ What are some of the decisions you've made that helped get you where you are now?

◊ Are you still running the agency, or are you doing something else?

Shortcuts to get started

Feeling stuck? Need more help? Here are some additional tips:

◊ **Start the Advance Retrospective with a future date.** For instance: "Today is Tuesday, December 31, 20XX. It's a great day because <such and such happened>."

◊ **Consider writing it as a walk-through of your day, as if you were writing a diary or journal entry that evening.** For instance: "I woke up, excited about finally <good thing>. After enjoying some caffeine in my comfortable home office, I had a short call with John about building a partnership with his company."

◊ **Use recollections to highlight what's different about this ideal future vs. today.** For instance: "I remember how I was always worried about finances. I now have a solid financial plan, and our checking account never goes below $X. It's so different from when I was worried about payroll."

◊ **Include big goals, but be realistic, too.** For instance, let's say one of your goals is to get more inbound leads. If you aren't getting *any* now, it might not make sense to write, "After just six months, we went from zero inbound leads a week to 100 leads a week." Instead, you might write, "We've tripled our inbound lead flow, and everyone's more qualified than ever before."

Work Less, Earn More

◊ **Write in multiple sessions.** It helps to take a break: Write until you feel stuck, then take a break. Go back a few days later and try again.

◊ **Make up names for people you don't work with yet but who'll be in your life in the future.** For instance, "I'm so glad I hired Sally as my COO. Her leading delivery means I can focus on growing the agency." This can help you identify the right person between now and then.

◊ **Accept that your ideal future may not include running your current agency.** We'll talk more about this in Chapter 2, but you *might* decide you want to exit. That's okay... and *Work Less, Earn More* will help.

When I work with coaching clients, most agency owners write Advance Retrospectives that are 1-3 pages in length, and it takes an hour or two (over a week or two). But you can write as much or as little as you want to. As a shortcut, read on for a template. Don't like writing? Record an audio or video version instead. Just keep *some* sort of record that you can look back on or listen to in the future.

Your Advance Retrospective—this first one, and updates in the months and years ahead—will help you stay on track and energize you for the journey ahead.

Okay, enough stalling. It's time to write your Advance Retrospective!

EXERCISE: Write a first draft of your five-year Advance Retrospective. Record your answers here, in a doc on your computer or phone, or in the corresponding page of the companion workbook.

My Advance Retrospective as of 20_____

Prompt: *Today is December 31, 20_____. It's a great day because...*

Keep writing... or take a break!

Start Planning Your Next Steps

Congrats on writing your first Advance Retrospective about where you'd like to be in the future! You'll refer back to this in the future—as a tool for clarity, delegation, and motivation.

But you're not done yet!

Visualizing the future isn't enough to get you there—you still need to create and implement a concrete plan. In the days ahead, here are some key questions to consider:

1. What obstacles will you need to overcome?

2. What's your preferred framework and growth style?

3. What are your top priorities in planning for the future?

4. What are some bite-sized steps you can take today?

5. How can you hold yourself accountable in making progress?

Ready to move forward? Use the workbook (including cut-and-paste templates). It's your bonus for buying this book; download the workbook at **WorkLessEarnMoreBook.com**

TL; DR
Chapter 1: Designing Your Ideal Agency
In a hurry? Here's what to know:

- To reach your ideal work less, earn more future, start by reflecting on your past: How has reality met and/or failed to meet your expectations?
- Visualize the future using an advance retrospective, a simple-yet-powerful tool to imagine where you want to be... so you can work backwards to get there. I recommend pretending it's five years from now.
- If you have business partners, each owner should complete the exercises in this book separately. Then, compare notes and reconcile the differences.
- Save a *lot* of time by using the tools in the free companion workbook. It'll help you make faster progress as you build out your "Work Less, Earn More" plan. (See, you're working less already!) You can download the workbook at **WorkLessEarnMoreBook.com**

Chapter 2:

The Four Stages of Day-to-Day Involvement

Are You Currently Mandatory, Necessary, Needed, and/or Optional?

In order to work less, you'll need to assess your level of involvement in each area of your business—and where you can scale it down. Then, you can start making that happen.

It's not a big secret on how to get there—it just takes knowing how to delegate work efficiently.

Work Less by Delegating

When you started—or joined—your agency, you were doing everything. As you've grown, you've built a team to take on more of the work. But it's hard to shake old habits, and what worked a year or two ago might not work today. That's why it's important to regularly evaluate your level of daily involvement in agency processes.

Consider **Landscape Leadership** founder and CEO **Chris Heiler**. He founded a growth marketing agency for green companies in the lawn and landscaping industry. Though his sales process worked, he knew it could be better. When he reached out for help, he was ready to "take things from a 6/10 to a 9/10."

I worked with him to create a method to better qualify his sales opportunities—one that Chris could delegate to his team. The agency grew revenue by raising its prices and growing the size of each client. They also stopped working with clients that weren't paying them enough each month. This allowed Chris to expand his team's responsibilities and stop personally doing things that weren't as critical for him as the owner.

Once the plan was implemented, things kept getting better—Chris cut his hours in half and doubled his income, netting record profit margins. Implementing just *one* process change led to bigger long-term results. And his team continues to use this process today with even larger clients.

So, **what could this look like for you?** Let's first review my four stages of day-to-day involvement for agency owners: Mandatory (Stage 1), Necessary (Stage 2), Needed (Stage 3), and Optional (Stage 4).

The Four Stages of Day-to-Day Involvement

In my experience, agency owners fall into four stages based on their day-to-day responsibilities. As you look through these, **think about which stage(s) you're in** *now*... **and which one(s) you** *want* **to be in**.

Depending on the topic, you may be in more than one at once—for instance, mandatory on sales but optional on project management.

Here's a visual model, in the form of a "fuel gauge":

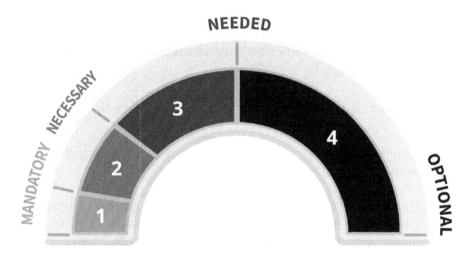

Let's take a closer look at each of the four stages to help you understand where you are now... and where you'd like to go.

Stage 1: Mandatory

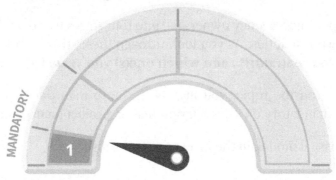

This is the stage most agency owners are familiar with—everyone starts off as **Mandatory**. In this stage, you are an integral part of your team's day-to-day decisions, whether because you *need* to be or because you *feel* like you can't let go.

Here are some signs that you might be mandatory (Stage 1):

◊ You can't get away for an *hour*—much less a few days—without something going wrong (and you certainly can't take a real vacation).

◊ You're interrupted all day long by both employees and clients. You're likely the primary contact for most, if not all, of your clients because you don't trust your team to handle them.

◊ It feels like you can never get your important work done— because you're constantly fighting fires at your agency.

◊ You rarely eat lunch on time... or if you do, the meal comes with a side of frantic multitasking and indigestion for dessert.

◊ Your significant other has stopped asking if you'll be working late, because they know the answer is "yes."

At this point, you're likely barely profitable—or even unprofitable. And you're certainly underpaid for the workload, stress, and negative impact on your life. But don't lose hope! Things get better as you progress to the second stage.

Stage 2: Necessary

Many agency owners find themselves at the **Necessary** stage. While it's certainly better than the mandatory stage, it's not a fun place to be.

When you're necessary, you're no longer mandatory to your team's day-to-day decisions—but you're still pretty involved.

Here are some signs you might be necessary (Stage 2):

◊ Even when you're not the primary client contact, you're still dragged in for firefighting a *lot* (more than once or twice a week).

◊ Your team is making decisions without you... but they're often *bad* decisions. Sometimes you hired the wrong people for the job—or you hired the right people, but they don't have the knowledge, resources, or access to make better decisions. And then you end up redoing the work yourself to fix mistakes.

◊ You might be able to take 2-3 days off, but a week or more seems impossible. And time off without checking email? No way.

At this point, your agency is *likely* profitable (up somewhat from mandatory). But assuming you're appropriately staffed, your net profit margins are likely *below* the healthy-agency benchmark of 20-30%.

When you make the upcoming jump from necessary to needed, you'll see a huge improvement to your quality of life. Things are about to get much better!

Stage 3: Needed

NEEDED

3

When you make yourself **Needed** (rather than necessary), your team is well-equipped to run things smoothly—often without your help. This is the minimum stage that most agency owners seek to achieve.

When you're needed (Stage 3):

◊ Your team is making decisions without you... and they're generally *good* decisions.

◊ You can take a week or two off without interruption. (It might take a couple tries, but you'll get there.)

◊ You're not stressed out all the time. And when you *are* stressed, you appreciate that it's not *constant,* as it once was.

◊ You can think strategically about your agency's future—and about how to ensure the business serves you, your family, your employees, and *their* families.

Needed doesn't mean you disappear *forever*, or that you can now work only 5-10 hours a week. You still need to set the vision, set long-term company goals, reinforce the culture, and so on. And you'll still need to be available for *some* day-to-day tasks as they come up. But you can set it, and forget it... for a while.

Most agency owners stop at this stage, especially if they lean toward running a lifestyle-oriented business. If you're happy with a one- or two-week vacation, that's fine. And if you're happy making an above-market salary, you can stay at needed. But some people want to go a step further...

Stage 4: Optional

This is the stage where some owners want to be—you can take a month away and not worry about the agency at all during that time. Your team is fully equipped to do the work without you, and you can choose to step in on day-to-day tasks where you prefer to (in a pre-planned way that doesn't disrupt your team's workflow).

Being **Optional (Stage 4)** also gives you the breathing room to focus *solely* on the fun stuff, however you define "fun"—maybe that's working on the vision, doing long-term planning, or focusing on company culture. You might also prepare for an exit, on your terms.

Is this the "be-all, end-all"? Not always. Some owners get to Optional and realize they're bored. They may choose to move back to the Needed stage in certain areas. Or they may decide to sell their agency and move on to the next thing—or early retirement.

Can you be in more than one stage at once?

Yes, absolutely. For instance, you might be optional on client delivery but mandatory or necessary on business development. Typically, you become less mandatory over time and as your agency grows.

__EXERCISE: Reflect on the following questions. Record your__ __answers here, in a doc on your computer or phone, or in the__ __corresponding page of the companion workbook. Download your__ __copy at WorkLessEarnMoreBook.com.__

Use the following stages to assess where you are now and where you'd like to be:

- ◆ *Stage 1: Mandatory*
- ◆ *Stage 2: Necessary*
- ◆ *Stage 3: Needed*
- ◆ *Stage 4: Optional*

Today: What's your *primary* current stage (or stages)? As a reminder, you can be in more than one stage at once—for instance, you might be optional on account management but mandatory for signing contracts.

Long-Term Future: What's your *ideal* stage? This may include being in more than one stage at once, depending on the level of involvement you *want* to have in different areas of your agency.

Work Less, Earn More

What It Means to Move Forward

In order to improve your quality of life, you'll need to move forward through the stages of involvement, from mandatory to necessary to needed... or even to optional.

When you make yourself needed but not necessary as a manager, your team still needs you for long-term direction and to sign off on big decisions. But you're not necessary for *every* decision—your team can make decisions without you, and they're generally good decisions.

That means you have time in your schedule to think strategically about your agency and take a week or two off each year without interruption. It means you're making an above-market salary and working reasonable hours so that you can have a life outside of work. And maybe even to go to optional.

But *how*? Now that we've covered *what* the stages are, let's look at *how* you can move through them.

How to Get to Your Ideal Stage

No matter where you are and where you want to be, the process for improving follows the same basic strategy. That is, you'll identify your current stage, set a goal for your next stage, create a plan to make the shift, execute the plan, and adjust based on the results.

As you prioritize, consider that certain techniques tend to make a big impact at certain steps. In fact, there's a specific tactic to help you make the jump from each specific page.

Here's a visual with details on each tactic:

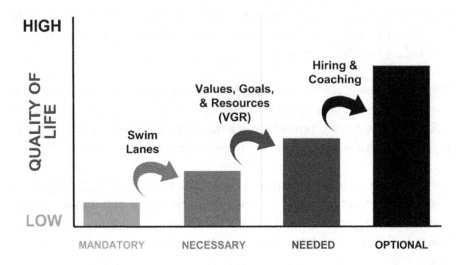

Now, let's look at how each jump might work.

Going from mandatory to necessary (Stage 1 to 2): Implement swim lanes

To go from mandatory to necessary, set and communicate the **"Swim Lanes"** your team should follow. This helps get things off your plate while minimizing duplicate work.

Swim Lanes are a shared definition of who's in charge of what. You know what they're handling, and they know what you're handling. And importantly, your *team* knows, too.

If everyone understands who owns what, people should stay out of each other's way—and they won't second-guess the responsible person's decisions. (The one exception is if the team's not meeting their goals— when things are slipping, it's reasonable to ask what's up.)

You can have swim lanes anywhere—with your employees, your business partners, and even your clients and sales prospects. Agreeing about roles and boundaries lets everyone focus on getting results—and helps you eliminate drama. In my experience, they're helpful any time you have two (or more) people who want to make decisions in a particular area. Ultimately, swim lanes work best if one person has the final responsibility in each area—they can get input and feedback, but it's ultimately their call. This helps agencies make progress instead of getting stuck arguing over who'll decide what.

Swim lanes can also address gray areas—for instance, defining that a PM can approve free client work up to $2,500 but needs higher-up approval to waive billables above that amount. There are fewer bottlenecks since the PM can handle most situations themselves—and then they know the person to escalate to if they need an override. A director might be able to waive up to $20,000. And then (depending on your hierarchy) higher amounts might require signoff from a VP, or a C-level executive, or finally you as the owner.

EXERCISE: Answer the following questions to help you start defining the Swim Lanes at your agency. This isn't a comprehensive list, but it'll get you thinking. Record your answers here, in a doc on your computer or phone, or in the corresponding page of the companion workbook.

Who's in charge of each client?

Who makes final decisions about certain client-strategy items?

Who makes decisions about design vs. technical vs. marketing considerations?

Who decides whether to provide "strategically free" work?

Who decides which project or retainer gets resources first?

Who's in charge of approving vacation and PTO requests?

Who decides which employee or contractor to hire?

What can contractors handle vs. what's employee-only?

What other large or small decisions come to mind?

Going from necessary to needed (Stage 2 to 3): Share your VGR with your team

To go from necessary to needed, ensure your team understands the relevant **"Values, Goals, and Resources" (VGR)** for each decision they're making—because then they don't need to ask you every time. This includes your agency's VGR, your VGR (as the owner), and each client's VGR.

What exactly *are* values, goals, and resources? It's the framework that allows other people to understand how to make decisions from *your* (or the agency's, or a client's) perspective. For example, if one of your values is that you won't work with nicotine clients, your team can auto-decline a sales inquiry from a new tobacco brand, instead of wondering what to tell the prospect (or interrupting you to ask what they should do).

Let's dive in a little deeper to each one of these as they work internally (and once you've figured out your internal VGRs, you can start using the framework externally, as well, for client work).

◊ **Agency-level Values:** At a high level, **you and your team should already know your agency's values**—it's part of the Mission, Vision, and Values (MVV) triplet. If you don't, you'll need to do some work to map those out. (It's worth spending time on this—it's easier to meet your goals when your team is on the same page.)

◊ **Agency-level <u>Goals</u>:** You and your management team have goals. **Do *all* of your employees know the agency-level goals?** If not, you'll want to fix that—otherwise, you risk having everyone pursuing different goals, and that's not going to help you succeed.

◊ **Agency-level <u>Resources</u>:** At its simplest, **do employees know what expenses they can incur without getting their manager's approval?** Giving everyone a decision-making budget means you (and your middle managers) won't get sucked into every choice. The expense budget doesn't have to be enormous—maybe it's $50 or $100 for a front-line employee and $500 or $2,500 (or any amount if recurring) for a director—but it means people feel empowered, and their manager isn't necessary for every small decision.

Beyond that, **do client-facing employees know the resources (budget, timeline, people) available as they work on client projects?** This shouldn't be a secret—when your team doesn't know the resources available, they either over-use resources (because they didn't know, and it hurts your margins) or they under-use resources (because they assumed they had fewer resources available, and quality suffers).

<u>**EXERCISE: What are your agency's Values, Goals, and Resources (VGR)? And what are *yours* individually, as the agency owner? Record your answers here, in a doc on your computer or phone, or in the corresponding pages of the companion workbook.**</u>

Your Agency-level VALUES (how you choose to operate):

Your Agency-level GOALS (where you want to go):

Your Agency-level RESOURCES (people, money, and tools to help you accomplish your goals):

Now take a moment to reflect on the values, goals, and resources that you hold as an agency owner—which might look different from your agency-level VGR! Keep these in mind when asking others to make agency decisions that reflect on you and your perspective.

Your Values as an Owner:

Your Short-Term Goals as an Owner:

Your Long-Term Goals as an Owner:

Your Resources as an Owner:

Work Less, Earn More

Going from needed to optional (Stage 3 to 4): Use hiring and coaching as tools

This leap in stages is about hiring and coaching—recruiting the right people and then sharing ongoing guidance to support them on continuous improvement.

Hiring and coaching employees goes beyond the scope of this book. But you can find more ideas in my book *Made to Lead: A Pocket Guide to Managing Marketing and Creative Teams* (available on Amazon), and my Agency Leadership Intensive program (learn more by visiting SakasAndCompany.com.)

TL; DR
Chapter 2: The Four Stages of Day-to-Day Involvement

In a hurry? Here's what to know:

- Start by assessing your level of involvement in each area of your business—and where you want to shift.
- Consider that most agency owners fall into four stages based on their day-to-day responsibilities (and may be in more than one at once—for instance, mandatory on sales but optional on PM).
- The four stages of day-to-day involvement are: 1) **Mandatory**, 2) **Necessary**, 3) **Needed**, and 4) **Optional**. For details, go back to the full chapter.
- Certain techniques tend to make a big impact in helping you move up a stage. Specifically:
  - To go from mandatory (Stage 1) to necessary (Stage 2): implement swim lanes, to clarify who's in charge of what.
  - To go from necessary (Stage 2) to needed (Stage 3): share your values, goals, and resources with your team, so they can make good decisions without asking you every time.
  - To go from needed (Stage 3) to optional (Stage 4): hire and coach the right people to build a stronger team.
- Access all of the tools and exercises mentioned here in the free companion workbook. You can download it at **WorkLessEarnMoreBook.com**.

Chapter 3:

Grow Your Support Team

Build the Foundation to Work Less and Earn More

Working less and earning more requires a solid foundation. What supports are in place to keep your agency not only running, but running *smoothly*? While designing your ideal future is important, that future won't be possible without key players to keep the wheels turning: **your team.**

Agency Success Starts with Your Team

Without a team, you don't have an agency.

If you neglect building, managing, and nurturing that team, you'll likely have problems in the future. Fortunately, the more you invest in building and managing a great team, the easier everything will be later.

Running an optimized agency team requires strategy, execution, and leadership.

Even with a top-tier MBA and years of business experience, **Liquid Spark** founder and president **Julie Thorner** experienced team-related challenges as she ran her agency.

As her business coach, I identified three key pain points that, when managed, would make things run more smoothly at Julie's adventure tourism agency:

1. Knowing *when* and *how* to delegate work,

2. Hiring the right staff, and

3. Creating easy-to-use templates and streamlined processes.

After we addressed those problems, Julie gained clear, efficient, and focused tools and processes. These help her onboard clients and additional staff and to do the self-marketing necessary to attract new clients.

Managing those initial pain points helped her nearly triple her revenue in three years, while boosting profitability. And she can now take an annual sabbatical, knowing her agency is running smoothly while she's away.

So, how do you work through *your* team management pain points? **Start by determining the ideal team composition for your agency.** This starts by understanding your role first, and then establishing ways your team can help.

Are You a Starter or a Finisher?

Agency owners tend to be either a **Starter** or a **Finisher**, but rarely both. What's the difference?

◊ If you're primarily a **Starter**, you're great at kicking things off. For instance, you might love sales and recruiting, or coming up with great ideas. But you need a finisher following behind you to turn those partially-baked ideas into reality (e.g., making sure that the agency gets a signed contract from that hot prospect, or creates a project plan for that great idea).

◊ If you're primarily a **Finisher**, you love turning concepts into reality. Your operations mindset turns the starter's big ideas into reality. You might not enjoy starting everything from scratch; odds are that you have a starter in your life to pass you the baton.

There's some overlap here with Gino Wickman's Entrepreneurial Operating System (EOS) concepts of "Visionaries" and "Integrators." But those two labels are more about high-level, big-picture strategy versus implementation. The starter and finisher concept is more about action.

Starters and finishers can *both* be visionaries, and they both take steps to integrate those visions. It's more about *where* in the process they prefer to do so—more on the front end or more on the back end.

Take a moment to reflect on which category *you* fall into. Based on that answer, you'll want to partner with people in the opposite category as you grow your agency.

Speaking of other people...

Create the Right Roles for Your Agency

Every agency has different needs, depending on the services you offer and how you approach internal operations. Your team structure should support your goals.

And, no—your team doesn't have to be 100% full-time employees. Part-time people count, as do freelancers. The main thing is that **you'll see more stability if it's a consistent team**. Consider eccentric 20th-century film director John Ford. He had a collection of actors and crew members he worked with over and over again. The stable working relationships helped Ford become one of the most important and influential filmmakers of his generation.

To set your agency up for success, it's important to build your own dream team. That team will help you work less and earn more—or help you stop working altogether if you choose.

A successful team is built up of specific types of roles, which fit into two categories: **agency roles** and **personal support roles**. Let's look at agency roles first.

Agency roles: Six categories for optimizing your agency

The right approach to team structure is unique to *your* agency, but there's a universal factor: **All agency roles fit into one of six categories.**

These categories are: account management (AM), project management (PM), subject matter expert (SME), client strategist, business development (BizDev), and support.

Once you understand these foundational roles, everything about running your agency gets easier. You can create the right jobs, hire the right people, communicate internally and externally, and manage your team for better results. Ultimately, knowing—and acting on—my six-category framework will help you make your agency more profitable.

If you're just starting out or running a smaller agency, *you* may be the one filling these roles. Or you might have team members whose work involves 2-3 roles at once; more on that shortly. As your agency grows, your team tends to become more specialized, so people can focus on what they do best.

My guidance on billables assumes a 40-hour workweek, where people are typically working ~47 weeks a year (after subtracting holidays and paid time off). If you observe something shorter—like a 35-hour workweek, or a version of a four-day workweek, or where people get far more PTO—you'll want to adjust your assumptions accordingly.

Let's consider a visual version of the model, and then details on each of the six categories.

Agency Roles Fit into These Six Categories

AM **Account Management:** Keep clients happy, and identify ways to expand the relationship.	**PM** **Project Management:** Deliver client projects and retainers smoothly and profitably.
SME **Subject Matter Expert:** Bill their "craft" (design, development, writing, analysis, etc.)	**Strategist** Recommend how to maximize each client's results, while staying within their budget.
BizDev **Marketing, Sales, and Partnerships:** Generate leads, close sales opps, and build partnerships.	**Support** **Operations & Leadership:** Ensure the business runs smoothly, on a short- and long-term basis.

Here's more on each of the six role categories, including typical job titles and weekly billable targets.

Account management (AM)

Account management (AM) keeps clients happy (and, typically, upsells them more work). This includes a focus on client retention as well as onboarding new clients. They are the voice of the client within the agency, ensuring the client is getting their needs met (although this sometimes leads to a well-meaning AM acting against the agency's interests).

Typical AM job titles include account manager, account director, account coordinator, and account specialist (although at some agencies, a "project manager" is more AM than PM). Sometimes an account director fits my AM category—but too often, it's a veiled salesperson title (and appears in BizDev, below).

I recommend an AM minimum billable target of 50%+ (that is, 20+ hours a week). They'll spend the rest of their time on non-billable relationship-building, upsells, and (at some agencies) outright sales. For more on sales, see the BizDev category below.

Project management (PM)

Project management (PM) completes work smoothly and profitably. They make sure things get done, primarily focusing on the internal team. "Project" is a misnomer; PMs can work on retainers and other recurring revenue. And at many agencies—especially smaller firms—PMs are client-facing, too.

Typical PM job titles include project manager, project coordinator, producer, traffic manager, resource manager, and director of PM. Some PMs tend to do some non-billable support work, too, in operations— especially if they're serving as a resource manager.

I recommend a PM minimum billable target of 50%+ (that is, 20+ hours a week). They'll spend their non-billable time on building internal processes, creating documentation, supporting sales estimates and proposals, and dealing with the overhead of "switching costs" as they shift between billable activities.

Subject matter expert (SME)

Subject matter experts practice a highly billable "craft." They're an expert in one or more areas, and their ideal day has them doing that thing all day long.

Although unique to each agency (and the services the agency provides to clients), typical SME job titles include designer, developer, copywriter, analyst, specialist, and QA technician.

Client strategists (below) are a special type of SME that's highly client-facing. Creative directors, art directors, and technical directors are each SMEs who have managerial (and sometimes sales support) responsibilities that reduce their billable targets.

Because AMs and PMs are ideally "protecting" SMEs from client interruptions, your SMEs should be billing 75-85% of their time (that is, 30-32 hours a week). I often see variations:

◊   An SME who also handles AM or PM will be lower, perhaps 60-70% billable. And a purely back-end SME (for instance, a developer or production designer who never talks to clients) could be 85-90% (32-36 hours a week), although that's rare.

◊   If an SME is a team lead (a senior team member who mentors and sometimes oversees other SMEs without being a pure manager), they'll have a somewhat lower billable target (because their job is to optimize others' billable time).

There's a role that seems like an SME, but it's really its own category: the client strategist. Why is it separate? Read on!

Client strategist

The client strategist role directs your agency to meet the client's goals by spending a client's budget on the highest-ROI activities. They're *technically* an SME (in the sense that they'd ideally do strategy—their craft—all day long). But since that necessarily requires client contact, think of client strategists as a mix of SME and AM.

Typical client strategist job titles include strategist, director of strategy, and VP of strategy. Be sure to insulate strategists from day-to-day client contact (via the AM and/or PM), since clients love talking to good strategists. That's *fine* if it meets the agency's needs... but not when the client strategist needs to be heads-down (especially if they need to be heads-down on a *different* client). Client strategists typically served in another SME role or as an AM before pursuing strategy.

Depending on how you've structured their role, a client strategist's billable target will be somewhere between an AM and a pure SME—

typically billing 60-75% (24-30 hours a week). Their non-billable time includes sales support, self-marketing support, and training other team members (including SMEs, AMs, and salespeople) on relevant trends. If the strategist is actually a salesperson, they're technically within the non-billable business development category (below).

Business development (BizDev): Marketing, sales, and partnerships

BizDev is about generating leads, working and closing sales opportunities, and building partnerships—various types of business-building work to bring in the billables that other team members ultimately fulfill. They're your internal self-marketers, salespeople, and (at forward-thinking agencies) partnership managers.

At agencies, typical BizDev job titles include director of marketing, marketing manager, business development representative, account executive, VP of growth, and partnerships manager.

If they're full-time, your BizDev people are typically 0% billable. Smaller agencies tend to have a mostly-billable person do some self-marketing. And at many agencies, the director of marketing is at least *partially* client-billable. Sometimes, account managers have a sales quota, too.

Support: Operations and agency leadership

Support staff make agency operations run smoothly—on both a short- and long-term basis. Your support team makes life easier for your billable team members, ensures the business *stays* profitable, and ensures clients pay on time.

As an owner, you're handling the agency leadership side of things. This includes setting the company vision, building agency culture, and everything else to keep things growing long-term.

Among employees doing operations, typical support job titles include executive assistant, office manager, operations manager, director of people, director of operations, VP of operations, and chief operating officer (COO). As agencies grow, owners tend to expand their support-related role(s) around business strategy for the agency itself.

Your agency's support people are typically 0% billable, although I'll sometimes see a 5-10% billable support person if they're helping the delivery team with quality assurance (QA). Relatedly, a resource manager will be at least partially billable when they coordinate people for billable work.

Why there isn't an "agency owner" role

As you can see, there isn't an "owner" role in my six role categories. Why? Because as the owner, your job is to do a mix of the six categories. And that mix shifts over time.

In the early days, you might be doing all six roles, and you might be mandatory (Stage 1) in almost all of them. Over time, you tend to focus on things like business development and client strategy, as you shift daily client work to others.

There isn't an "owner" role because there's no *one* way to be an owner. In some ways, that's scary—and in other ways, it's freeing. You can craft your role to be the role you want.

What about agency structure?

Your agency structure is very important. For instance, should you use a flat model, a functional (hierarchical) structure, pods, or something else?

Customizing your agency structure is beyond the scope of this book. Flat models tend to break as you grow, but they're fine if you don't plan to grow beyond 10-12 people. Meanwhile, pods can make it easier to scale-up... but you need to optimize the client load and team size for each pod, and decide how to handle cross-pod roles.

Making compromises: When you need someone to do two or three roles at once

It's common for newer or smaller agencies to overlap roles. In some cases, **employees might serve in two or three roles at once**. So, which roles *can* be combined successfully?

Here are some common wearing-multiple-hats combos I see at agencies—along with the and pros and cons for each combination.

◊ **AM + Strategist:** The day-to-day client contact also creates the client's long-term strategy. Clients like having continuous access to their strategist. But clients are less likely to respect strategy advice from the person handling the account's day-to-day nuts and bolts (and in my experience, clients rarely want strategy advice from a PM).

◊ **AM + SME:** The client contact also does the execution work. This is the norm within PR agencies, where the AM is also doing SME work like media relations, writing copy, and placing press releases. I see it at many pay-per-click agencies, too—where the person running campaigns is also the client's direct contact. Clients like the access, but agencies tend to make a compromise: an AM-oriented person may not be a great SME, or an SME doesn't love that clients keep interrupting their "maker" time. (More on that in Chapter 6.)

◊ **AM + PM:** The client's day-to-day contact is also coordinating everything with the internal team. This is efficient—because there's less lost in translation between client requests and the internal task assignments. But it's not always effective, since employees tend to lean toward either keeping clients happy (AM) or doing work as-scoped (PM), they usually do well in one role and poorly in the other. Having been in this combo role earlier in my career, I strongly recommend splitting this role ASAP. It helps you avoid problems around client retention and employee retention.

◊ **PM** + **Support:** Someone does internal coordination and operations. It's usually a good match, because PMs and operations people tend to have the same detail-oriented profile. I did this as an agency operations manager—where I intentionally reduced my client work and increased my internal operations work. The risk is that client work can easily distract from internal work, or vice versa.

◊ **AM** + **BizDev:** It's normal for AMs to focus on upsells with existing clients. But in this combination, AMs also do sales for new business. The biggest risk is that employees ignore current clients in favor of sales opportunities, or vice versa. Be extra-careful about incentive alignment if you choose this combo.

◊ **AM** + **PM** + **Strategist:** I did this combination as a director of client services at a small agency. It's not ideal because it's hard to think about client relationships *and* internal coordination *and* client strategy all at once. As I took on support (operations) responsibilities, we hired an account coordinator to handle AM and PM on our smaller accounts, while I continued to support client strategy. It was a lot of juggling.

These combinations often exist out of necessity, rather than desire—you know it's better to have specialists, but you can't currently afford to hire more people.

As you grow, you'll want to separate the roles so that people can specialize—from three to two categories, and from two categories to just one. This helps people focus on what they do best, which helps you grow your agency.

Your turn: What do these six roles look like at *your* agency?

Before you can strategize how to work less, you'll need to take stock of your current team. Where are the gaps in your agency's capacities and capabilities? Where can roles be restructured or streamlined for maximum efficiency across the team?

The following exercise will help you visualize the changes you need to make in your existing structure, and where you might need to grow your team. Can't currently afford a great team? Use this exercise to build out your future team needs.

EXERCISE: Reflect on the following questions. Record your answers here in the book, in a doc on your computer or phone, or in the corresponding page of the companion workbook. Download your copy at WorkLessEarnMoreBook.com.

Start by doing an "inventory" of the roles at your agency. Who's doing what? Are there any roles where it's unclear who's in charge? How many people are doing more than one role? Is anyone doing more than 2-3 roles?

Reflect on how you might split or shift roles, especially where you notice current gaps. For instance, if you like client strategy but don't want to be the client's day-to-day contact, you'll need to recruit someone to handle AM. If the person doing PM isn't detail-oriented, you'll want to shift that to someone who *is*.

Reflect on how your team *structure* needs to change as you grow. The structure that worked a year ago likely won't work a year from now... and it may not be working today. What do you need to shift to help the agency serve you? For instance, is it time to shift from function-based teams to a pod structure, or a partial pod structure?

Now, beyond the six Agency Role categories, let's look at your *extended* team. I call these your "personal support" roles.

Personal support roles: Build your network

Successful business leaders rely on a team of advisors for specialized guidance on agency leadership, taxes, health, and more.

In my work with agency owners, **the highest performers have an advisory team**—going beyond their key employees and freelancers. As a coach, I'm one of their advisors—but rarely their *only* advisor.

You technically don't *require* outside advisors. But if you want to work less and earn more, your advisory team can help you reach your professional and personal goals faster and more smoothly than if you worked on your own.

I've identified 12 key advisory roles for you to consider—and as a business owner, I have nearly all of them myself (spanning more than a dozen people). Keep in mind that not all of them will be tax-deductible; speak with your tax advisor to understand how to pay people in your specific situation.

Use this list to consider what areas of support might help you succeed as an agency owner. The smoother your personal life, the easier it is to succeed at your agency.

Coach(es)

Coaching is about accountability and advice to help you reach your goals as quickly, smoothly, and profitably as possible. I've had a life coach for nearly a decade and previously worked with a sales coach. They make a big impact, both professionally and personally.

For my clients, I'm their executive coach, with a focus on agency-specific business and leadership advice. (Keep in mind that some coaches don't give advice; for instance, my approach is technically consulting-style coaching.)

But coaching alone may not give you everything you need. Consider therapy, too.

Therapist

I've been in therapy off and on for more than two decades, and it's been very helpful. Unlike your close friends, a therapist is a neutral party with training to help you work through underlying issues that get in your way. In-person is helpful, but teletherapy can be more convenient. If your mental health involves medication, you may need to engage a psychiatrist as well.

Executive assistant (EA)

Having an assistant makes your day-to-day life easier. Technically, they're a member of your agency team, in the support category we discussed earlier. But the best assistants also serve as an advisor. That is, they're sharing insights to help you improve—including "intelligent disobedience," where they diplomatically push back if you request something that doesn't make sense.

If you can't afford to hire a full-time EA, consider delegating to a part-time virtual assistant (VA) first. Read more on that in Chapter 10.

Lawyer(s)

At a minimum, you should have a general business lawyer. A former boss had three lawyers on-call: a contracts attorney, an HR specialist, and a litigator. That's probably overkill; your attorney can refer you to a specialist when needed. I've worked with several law firms, two of which specialize in helping agencies.

HR consultant

You need someone advising on specific legal issues for your team, including local regulations. Your HR consultant is a more-affordable option than a lawyer for day-to-day issues. If you use a professional employer organization (PEO) for co-employment, they'd likely handle HR consulting.

Personal trainer

If you love working out and can create your own program, you don't need a personal trainer. In my case, I *don't* enjoy working out—so personal training sessions turn the workout into a meeting... and I don't skip meetings. I'm currently between trainers; my previous trainer worked with me in-person, and then we switched to remote sessions.

Financial planner

I work with a fee-only certified financial planner (CFP) who's also a registered investment advisor (RIA). That means they act as a fiduciary, where they put my interests before their own. I also like that they use a coaching-style approach designed to support my life goals, rather than handling finances in a vacuum.

Accountant and/or tax advisor

Don't do your own taxes! A good accountant and/or a tax advisor will pay for themselves in tax savings and/or headache-reduction. When I had an international tax question a few years ago, I got one-off advice from a tax attorney. Day-to-day, my business CPA's firm also does my personal taxes (paid separately), which makes it easier to integrate the advice.

Insurance agent

Insurance is important, complicated... and best left to the experts. There's no one-size-fits-all approach to insurance for agencies, and you might need more than one insurance agent. Having a trustworthy business insurance agent will make it easier to navigate all your options. Your agent also advocates for you when you have a difficult claim.

Banker

You might not expect hands-on customer service for your personal banking... but you need it in your business. Your business banker can help you access loans or a line of credit. And they can escalate internal problem-solving if something goes wrong.

Nutritionist

What you eat makes a big impact on how you feel, which impacts your productivity as an agency owner. Sometimes you can get nutrition advice through a personal trainer or life coach, but you might prefer a dietician or other specialist. Don't forget sleep hygiene, too.

Spiritual advisor

A spiritual advisor can enhance your life journey in ways others just can't. They might support you on an unpaid basis, or you might hire a spiritual coach. I don't have a dedicated spiritual advisor, but I get support in this area from others on my advisory team.

Your turn: What personal support do you need?

Having a solid personal support team is crucial for your wellbeing, which ultimately affects how you show up for your agency. When you have the support you need to run a well-organized agency, your team will thrive. And if you're in a relationship, your spouse or partner will be glad that it doesn't all fall on them.

Personal support looks different for everyone. You may not need all 12 categories listed here, or you might add others. Take a moment to reflect on what your current network looks like, including additional support you need to help you work less and earn more.

What does your current personal support network look like?

What roles are filled and which are missing?

What are your next steps to fix any gaps?

Don't Forget the Infrastructure!

Great people can't do great work if they're working in a broken system. You need *infrastructure*. The right systems come down to **processes, policies, and software**:

◊ **Processes:** Are team members clear on the processes to follow? Do you need to level-up or otherwise change your existing processes? Do you need to *create* them in the first place? (But don't update these *too* often, or your team won't know which is current.)

◊ **Policies:** Are team members clear on the policies to follow? Policies include your employee handbook and guidelines for clients. Those include client contracts, statements of work, promises about turnaround time, etc.

◊ **Software:** This includes PM tools, accounting software, time-tracking, role-specific tools (e.g., graphic design, development environment, ad management), CRM and marketing automation, sales proposals, etc. It also may include all-in-one agency management software (but beware: this approach works best when everyone uses it 100% of the time).

The *exact* processes, policies, and software to create and use are beyond the scope of this book. But be sure to prioritize getting them right. And dedicate time to maintain the systems to ensure they *keep* working.

Later, we'll talk about enlisting your team—but next, let's look at how you'll create the plan to do so.

TL; DR
Chapter 3: Grow Your Support Team
In a hurry? Here's what to know:

- Success starts with your team. Running an optimized agency requires strategy, execution, and leadership.
- Determine if you're a starter or finisher. Starters enjoy coming up with big ideas and kicking them off; finishers like turning those ideas into reality.
- The six agency roles are: account management (AM), project management (PM), subject matter expert (SME), client strategist, business development (BizDev), and support.
- The 12 personal support roles are: coach(es), therapist, executive assistant (EA), lawyer(s), HR consultant, personal trainer, financial planner, accountant and/or tax advisor, insurance agent, banker, nutritionist, and spiritual advisor.
- Do an inventory of the roles at your agency and in your personal support network. Who's doing what? What roles are unclear and which are missing?
- Great people can't do great work with a broken system. The right infrastructure systems come down to processes, policies, and software.
- Access all of the tools and exercises mentioned here in the free companion workbook. You can download it at **WorkLessEarnMoreBook.com**.

Chapter 4:
Work Less

Leveling-up From Mandatory to Necessary to Needed to Optional (Stages 1-2-3-4)

You've written your advance retrospective about your ideal future. You've identified what needs to change to help you reach that ideal future. And you've looked at your team. Now, it's time to choose and deploy strategies for *getting* there!

In this chapter, we'll talk about work less—and in the next chapter, we'll talk about earn more.

Get Ahead of Problems

First up on the path to working less? Having the right strategies for problem solving. These won't *instantly* get you from 80 hours a week to 40 hours a week, but they'll help you head in the right direction.

The best way to solve problems? Prevent them in the first place! And that often starts by doing a "pre-mortem."

Do a Pre-Mortem

You can prepare by doing a **"pre-mortem."** Essentially, this is a debrief you do *before* things start. Pre-mortems work for client engagements and internal initiatives.

As with debriefs (or "post-mortems"), you'll make a list of all the things that can go wrong... as well as what can go *right*. Yes, you read that correctly: Being wildly successful can cause its own problems.

For example, consider raising your agency's prices (something to create room to help you work less and earn more).

◊ **What could go wrong?** Your largest client isn't happy about the increased cost of your services... and decides to fire your agency.

◊ **What could go (too) right?** A nuisance client agrees to pay the higher rate you thought they'd say "no" to... but the new rate *still* isn't high enough to make it worthwhile.

Neither of these situations is ideal, but being prepared for them ahead of time will help you prevent them happening in the first place (or have a plan of action ready if they *do* happen).

Of course, not everything in your pre-mortem merits an in-depth follow-up—part of working less is you don't have to plan for *every* contingency.

Instead, I recommend preparing for two categories: what's **likely**, and what's **catastrophic**.

◊ If a scenario is **likely to happen**, you should probably prepare for it... because it's likely to happen.

◊ If a scenario is *unlikely* to happen—but it would be **catastrophic** if it *did*—you'll want to create a plan for that scenario, too.

Preparing pre-mortems with your team can help you discover potential future problems and keep you from repeating the same mistakes over and over again.

Okay, it's your turn. Open the Advance Retrospective you created earlier, about your ideal future. In getting there, what could go wrong? What could go right? Use the space below to create your pre-mortem.

EXERCISE: Reflect on the following questions, with an eye toward the Advance Retrospective you wrote earlier, about your ideal future. Record your answers here in the book, in a doc on your computer or phone, or in the corresponding page of the companion workbook. Download your copy at WorkLessEarnMoreBook.com.

Assume your Advance Retrospective has mostly happened… except that something went horribly wrong along the way. That is, it's *not* your ideal future. **Describe *what* went wrong.**

***Why* did things go wrong?** What happened? Who was involved?

Now, assume things went *really* well. That is, your future turned out even *better* than you ever thought would happen. **What problems would *this* create?**

Why **did those problems happen?** Who was involved?

Now, come back to the present. **What can you do differently *today* to prevent things from falling apart in the future?** How can you ensure things go smoothly?

Take Back Your Time

Whether you're looking to work less by reducing your hours or by increasing the *quality* of the hours you work, it's important to understand how you're currently spending your time. This helps you determine which members of your team can help—and identify people you need to hire to take on those responsibilities.

To get your unique answer, let's do an exercise from my consulting and coaching work to troubleshoot where things are now. I call it the "Time Bucket" process. (Coming up in a few pages, via the companion workbook, I'll share a template for this.)

Think about your time in different buckets: long-term agency strategy, sales and bizdev, managing your team, administrative, etc. How much time are you spending on each bucket? How much time would you *ideally* like to be spending on each?

Maybe you're currently spending 50% of your time on client billables, but ideally you'd like to cut it out of your workload entirely—and spend that time working on team culture instead. The shift will make you happier in your daily work life, and it ultimately benefits the agency as a whole.

Now that you know, you can take action.

Consider agency owner **Dale Bertrand**. He's the founder and president of **Fire&Spark**. Like many agency owners, Dale was stretched to manage his agency's needs, stuck spending time and energy on work that didn't contribute to growth. He reached out for my coaching support.

First, we identified that his day-to-day involvement in client billables was taking up 80% of his week—which didn't leave space to plan or execute on long-term agency strategy. By making shifts to cut this to a light 10%, Dale created space to fix problems that hurt agency growth. And he eliminated his long-running night-and-weekend work, creating time to spend with his family.

By repositioning *how* he was spending his time at work, Dale raised Fire&Spark's retainer fees by 34%, improved client retention, and lowered his stress levels. Now, Dale can focus on the sales and marketing activities he enjoys most—and which continue contributing to the agency's growth.

Want to see similar results at your agency? Start by finding my **Time Bucket Template** in the companion workbook. This tool will help you visualize the shifts you need to make in taking control over your time. List the percentage of time you spend in key areas, and then the percentages you *want* those to be. As you compare the numbers, add your initial observations on how you might make the increase or decrease happen.

EXERCISE: Fill out the Time Bucket Template in the companion workbook. You'll look at where you're spending time now, what you want that to become in the future, and where to start making changes first.

Create S.M.A.R.T.-er Goals

It's not enough to just say, "I want to grow my agency." To make it actually *happen*, **you need to make every goal a S.M.A.R.T. goal**. That includes your own goals, as well as the goals you delegate to your team.

Whether the goals are big or small, the S.M.A.R.T. framework keeps everyone on the same page—and helps you get things done faster and more profitably. **Let's take a deeper look at what this means, and how to apply it at your agency.**

Definition: What are S.M.A.R.T. goals?

As a goal-setting framework, **S.M.A.R.T.** is an acronym to help everyone understand what "done" means. The letters stand for:

◊ **Specific.** The goal clearly conveys what you're trying to accomplish.

◊ **Measurable.** You can quantify the results.

◊ **Assignable.** You can assign the goal to someone... or to yourself.

◊ **Realistic.** The goal is achievable (based on the current resources and other circumstances), rather than impossible or improbable.

◊ **Time-bound.** There's a deadline, so you know whether you finished the goal on time.

Let's look at an example, to help you apply this at your agency.

Example: Turning a non-S.M.A.R.T. goal into a S.MA.R.T. goal

When someone tells me they want to grow their agency, I have a lot of questions—including how much, by when, and the size of their current baseline.

Likewise, **you might initially say, "I want to grow my agency."** That's a good goal, but it's not a S.M.A.R.T. goal. Fortunately, we can fix that!

The changes are relatively straightforward, and the process gets easier with practice.

Here's how to turn "I want to grow my agency" into a S.M.A.R.T. goal:

◊   Make it **Specific**: So, you want to grow your agency—but *what* are you growing? Revenue? Net profits? Your personal income from the agency? Be specific and choose. For instance, you might choose to grow your revenue from billables. Now, it's *specific*: We're talking about billables, not pass-through revenue like printing costs or media spend.

◊   Make it **Measurable**: Your revenue-growth goal might be to grow billables from $4 million today to $10 million. Great! But you still need to determine what metrics you'll use to track this. How will you measure your progress? How will you know when the goal is accomplished? Choose your metrics... then get it off of your plate.

◊   Make it **Assignable**: Who's your go-to person at the agency to help you achieve this? Increasing revenue can't fall solely to you. Delegating spreads the goal across the agency, with the team working toward the same result. Look back at your Time Bucket Template for some ideas here. For example, you might assign "grow billables from $4 million to $10 million" to your COO. And then they might assign components of that goal to their subordinates. But that raises another consideration...

◊   Make it **Realistic**: Are you trying to grow from $4 to $10 million in one year? That's... unlikely. The definition of "realistic" is unique to each agency—but it ultimately needs to be determined. Are you trying to grow that over 10 years? Three years? If you said, "Grow from $4 to $10 million in billables over three years," it *might* be realistic—but it depends on your ability to fulfill that growth. Achieving 36% annual growth for three years requires a strong marketing and sales pipeline, sales abilities, and a capacity to deliver the work. What would it take to make that all happen?

◊   Make it **Time-bound**: Set a deadline. In this revenue-growth example, tell your COO the date you expect to achieve growing annual billable-based revenue from $4 million to $10 million. Think about whether this goal is achievable in the short term, or whether it's part of a long-term strategy. For example, you might create a short-term plan for progress on revenue in the next 1-2 years, as you work toward your 5- or 10-year goal.

Want to take it up a notch? Consider extending your efforts to create S.M.A.R.T.I.E. goals. Here, the "I" is for "Inclusion" (ensuring everyone feels valued and included) and the "E" is for "Equity" (treating people equally).

Your turn: Create an agency S.M.A.R.T. goal

Now that you understand how to create achievable goals, let's put this into practice! Review your Advance Retrospective and consider the goals you're trying to achieve. Then, use the exercise below to turn one of them into a S.M.A.R.T. goal.

EXERCISE: Create a S.M.A.R.T. goal for your agency's long- or short-term strategy. Record your answers here, in a doc on your computer or phone, or in the corresponding page of the companion workbook.

What's a goal that you're working toward?

What would make it more...

- **S**pecific?

- **M**easurable?

- **A**ssignable?

- **R**ealistic?

- **T**ime-bound?

Put it all together: **Re-write your goal as a S.M.A.R.T. goal:**

Consider: How Will Your Working Less Impact Your Team?

If you're working less... that usually means *someone* will be working more. And that someone is generally your team.

We've talked a lot in the last couple of chapters about delegating work—which is crucial for your ability to work less—but it's important to make sure you're delegating *responsibly*.

Delegation is *not* abdication. Make sure you're not just dumping all the work on your team without considering how much capacity they currently have. After all, an overworked team is more likely to quit... And high turnover means you'll ultimately be working more.

Part of your plan to work less, earn more may include hiring additional people (employees and/or contractors) to handle the workload you delegate. This increases expenses short-term, but it's an investment toward your long-term goals.

And consider: **Your team may *welcome* new responsibilities, if these help them reach their career development goals.** My clients typically promote key employees as the employees expand their role. I've done that, too—it's important that your "Work Less, Earn More" program benefits your team, too.

There's more in Chapter 5 on working with your team. For now, consider how they'll be involved as you start your "work less" plan.

Use Quick Wins to Stay Motivated for Long-Term Success

Planning long-term goals can be exciting as you look to your ideal future... but it can also be frustrating to feel like you're not seeing progress in the short term.

Big changes take time. Fortunately, there are things you can do in the next week or month to accelerate your progress and keep you motivated.

I call these straightforward, short-term tasks "Quick Wins." There are plenty you can choose from within your own agency. Here are just a few examples.

Quick Win #1: Ask sales prospects to complete a pre-qualification survey before you do a call

Have you (or one of your salespeople) gotten on a call with a prospect who turned out to be a terrible fit? Avoid that common problem by asking clients to complete a pre-qualification survey before you get on the phone.

This can help you shorten your exploratory calls—and skip doing a call altogether if someone clearly isn't a fit. The pre-questionnaire doesn't have to be too in-depth, either; consider starting with 5-7 questions.

You can always adjust the list, based on what the feedback you receive from prospects and your team.

Quick Win #2: Require clients to complete a pre-kickoff survey

Have you (or a colleague) ever led a kickoff meeting where you realized client stakeholders weren't on the same page with each other—or they expected you to do work you never agreed to do? Yeah, me too.

My solution is to do a pre-kickoff survey before the kickoff meeting. You'll ask each stakeholder about what they expect, how they define success, and how much time they expect your work will take each week.

When there's a mismatch—between your plans or between stakeholders—you now have an opportunity to address this before things blow up. Plus, you'll often identify upsell opportunities for later.

Quick Win #3: Define Swim Lanes for your management team

Do you keep thinking to yourself, "Why are you asking me? That's your job!"? Are you running into disagreements about who's in charge of what—or things aren't happening because no one's in charge? Are people getting frustrated because other people keep barging into their decision making?

If any of those scenarios sounds familiar, it's time to define swim lanes. Just as a swimming pool has dividers between lanes—so that swimmers stay in their own lane—your agency will benefit from creating (and maintaining, and adapting) work swim lanes.

Look back at Chapter 2 for guidance on creating swim lanes.

You can use an A.R.C.I. (or R.A.C.I.) matrix to organize your swim lanes, by clarifying four roles for each task or decisionmaking area: **A**ccountable, **R**esponsible, **C**onsulted, and **I**nformed. For more on this, see Chapter 6.

Other options for Quick Wins

Those three examples may not be the right ones for you, or may not be the right ones at the moment. The right Quick Wins will depend on the underlying issues that exist at your agency.

For instance, you might choose to implement a client satisfaction survey or use an employee engagement tool to identify internal dissatisfaction before it becomes a problem.

Whatever you do, **don't jump to do all of these at once**. Pick 1-2 to start, and then move on to others.

Ideally, you'll delegate these to your management team to lead. For example:

1. Give your directors a timeline and any other resource constraints.

2. Schedule interim check-ins to review progress.

3. Let them take the lead on making the quick wins happen.

Your leaders will feel good about what they've accomplished, and you'll benefit from the results—without getting sucked into doing everything yourself. It's a nice way to start moving toward work less.

Now it's time for you to try it!

EXERCISE: Pick a Quick Win for the upcoming week (or month) and implement a plan to get it done. Record your plan here, in a doc on your computer or phone, or in the corresponding page of the companion workbook.

Later in the book, I'll share further tips to help you work less. But in the next chapter, we'll review what it takes to earn more.

TL; DR
Chapter 4: Work Less
In a hurry? Here's what to know:

- Get ahead of problems by doing pre-mortems to identify scenarios that need a contingency plan.
- Identify the buckets where you're spending most of your time (e.g. sales and BizDev, managing your team, administrative, etc.) and where you would *like* to be spending your time. How might you make those increases or decreases happen?
- Implement the S.M.A.R.T. framework at your agency to create goals that are: Specific, Measurable, Assignable, Realistic, and Time-bound.
- Consider how your working less will impact your team. Delegate, don't abdicate!
- Look for Quick Wins— straightforward, short-term tasks that accelerate your progress and keep you motivated while you implement long-term change. Pick 1-2 at a time and celebrate as you complete them—all progress is good progress!
- Access all of the tools and exercises mentioned here in the free companion workbook. You can download it at **WorkLessEarnMoreBook.com**.

Chapter 5:
Earn More

Are You Making Enough? (Hint: Probably Not.)

Think about your agency as a business. Are you being adequately compensated for the risks involved in running the company? Are you able to pay your team what they deserve? Is what you're earning enough to meet your short- and long-term goals and fund your ideal future?

If the answer to any of those questions is "no," **you're not making enough money**, regardless of how "comfortable" you might feel about where you currently are.

So, let's help you earn more!

Agencies vary dramatically in size and structure. In this chapter, I'll speak to examples from my own experience as an agency consultant: independent, owner-operated agencies with fewer than 100 employees, serving clients primarily in the developed world.

If that describes your situation, these examples are likely to apply to you. And if your situation is different, consider how you might adapt the advice to your agency.

How Much You Could Be Making

For most independent agencies, **an agency owner ideally pays themselves between $150,000 and $500,000 a year in salary...** plus other rewards.

◊ There's technically no limit on how much you can pay yourself—but in practice, I rarely see payroll-based salaries that are above $500,000. (With shareholder distributions, you could hit $1 million, $2 million, or more.)

◊ If you're paying yourself *less* than $150,000 today—because you started your agency recently, or you're following intentional guidance from your tax advisor—that's okay. You can look for ways to grow your income as you grow your agency.

Beyond salary, you'll likely owe taxes on annual pass-through profits—regardless of whether you take the profits in cash. Even as you take cash distributions to cover your personal taxes (and other personal priorities), you'll likely reinvest a portion of profits back into the business.

You may be looking at that $150,000 to $500,000 range and think it's *big*. **Where should you fall within that range, based on your agency's size and revenue?**

Fortunately, there are nine key factors to help you decide what's right for you... and to check whether you might be under-paid.

Let's look at the factors.

Nine factors: Adjusting owner compensation to your situation

In my work across hundreds of agencies, I've identified nine factors that impact owner compensation at independent agencies. Consider:

1. **Agency revenue:** The higher your revenue, the more you can afford to pay yourself. If you want to pay yourself $1 million but your total revenue is $1 million... that's just not going to happen (yet). But more revenue doesn't guarantee higher owner compensation because some agencies grow unprofitably rather than profitably.

2. **Profit margins:** Ideally, you're getting 20-30% net profit margins after paying everyone market-rate compensation or higher. Most agencies operate as pass-through entities, meaning the owners pay taxes individually based on the business profits rather than the business paying taxes on profits. The higher your profits, the larger a shareholder draw you'll likely take, to cover the tax bill for your on paper profits. But you don't hang onto those for-taxes distributions.

3. **Co-owners:** You and any business partner(s) tend to be the highest-paid people at the agency. More partners mean more owner compensation—leaving less money to pay non-owner employees. In practice, agencies tend to spend 50-60% of revenues on labor (including owner, employee, and key contractor compensation). If you overpay the owners there's no money left to pay everyone else. And you probably don't want to do *all* the work yourself.

4. **Geographic cost of living:** Living in a city like New York, London, or Singapore is more expensive than living in a small town or a mid-sized city. You'll likely adjust your owner compensation up or down to reflect that reality.

5. **Full-time vs. part-time:** Most agency owners are working full time in the agency (that is, 40+ hours a week). As the owner, you always have the option to work less than full time—but you probably won't pay yourself 100% of your previous compensation

because some of that money will go to pay a successor to do your old job(s).

6. **Tax planning:** Your tax advisor may recommend a (relatively) low salary for tax purposes—but there are limits to that strategy. For benchmarking, consider converting your compensation to a salary-based equivalent to make this an apples-to-apples comparison.

7. **Personal preference:** Owners tend to pay themselves to support their lifestyle expectations, which vary dramatically. Some agency owners have a second home, a healthy travel budget, or annual tuition expenses. Others are minimalists. These choices impact your agency's growth, recruiting, and profits—and the owner's quality of life. For instance, consider whether you're a Maximizer or an Optimizer. (Unsure which one you are? Re-read that section in the Introduction.)

8. **Sales pipeline:** Agency owners with more recurring revenue tend to feel more confident about paying themselves a higher salary. To grow your income, be sure to build your agency's marketing and sales pipeline, and consider growing—or securing—your recurring revenue.

9. **Self-confidence:** Some agency owners don't feel they're worth paying themselves more—this is usually a sign of imposter syndrome. Sound familiar? If so, I suggest reading *Overcoming Underearning* by Barbara Stanny. You may also find it helpful to check in with peers in similar positions, or talk to a therapist or other advisor to get some perspective.

That's not entirely it, though. There's one more factor to consider as you think about how much you should be paying yourself: what you'd need to do if you were 100% optional at the agency.

Bonus factor: What would it cost to replace you?

To ensure you're paying yourself enough, consider how much you'd need to pay someone else to replace you.

If you were to bring someone in to lead things—as a CEO, president, or managing director—they would need to be well compensated for the responsibility they carry in running your agency. After all, it's a difficult and often stressful job.

How well compensated? This typically translates to a six-figure base salary, plus profit-sharing bonus and other incentives. I often see between $120,000 and $200,000. Sometimes that hits $250,000, although I rarely see a cash portion above $300,000 for a hired non-owner CEO.

If you're not paying yourself at *least* as much as you'd pay your replacement, consider increasing your salary.

Whether you keep your role or hire a replacement, you'll need to identify *how* to pay yourself more (or pay your TBD replacement enough to make them want the job). Here are some general categories:

→ Salary

→ Draw (shareholder distributions, if they're an owner)

→ Bonuses

→ Commissions

→ Benefits

→ Expense reimbursement

→ Phantom stock (if they're not a formal owner)

The next step? Actually increasing how much you're paying yourself. Let's consider your options.

Three Ways to Increase Your Income

You've decided to increase your pay—whether through salary, draw, bonuses, or something else. But now you need to decide where the money should come from. You've got three options, and you might choose to do one, two, or potentially all three of them:

◊ **Option A: Pay yourself more now out of existing profit margins.** If your net profit margins exceed 30%, you have room to pay yourself more. And if they're above 20%, you likely have some room, too. But what if your margins aren't there? Then it might be time to...

◊ **Option B: Grow your top-line revenue.** More revenue *theoretically* means more money is there to pay you. We'll talk about strategizing for revenue growth in later chapters, but keep in mind that you may choose to do this in conjunction with...

◊ **Option C: Grow your margins through higher productivity.** That is, your team produces more revenue by working more productively and efficiently.

Increasing productivity should be a goal for *all* agency owners seeking to run an efficient agency. But when you want to work less and earn more, this step is crucial. Investing in your team's competence and capability sets the stage for your agency's success—and by extension, your success.

Levers to increase agency productivity

First, keep in mind that **labor typically consumes 50-60% of your revenue**. That includes employees, ongoing contractors, and you, the owner (or owners). Some agencies spend more than 60% on labor, which means their profit margins are going to be lower than 20-30%.

If you're paying *less* than 50% for labor—unless you are primarily outsourcing work to countries with a low cost of living—you may be understaffed. For example, a new client in Australia reported spending only 30-35% on labor... because (it turned out) they were trying to personally fulfill a $20,000 a month retainer. That was not sustainable.

Regardless of your billing model—whether it's time and materials, deliverable-based, or value-based—**your team's time is your "inventory" to sell**. The more of that inventory they bill, the higher your productivity... and the higher your profit margins.

Consider agency owner **Chris Dreyer**. Chris is the founder and CEO of **Rankings.io**, a specialist agency for law firms nationwide. His agency had reached $2 million in annual sales, and Chris wanted to keep the momentum going and maintain his growth trajectory.

He thought the only way to do that was to increase his client load significantly. When he reached out for help, I encouraged him to see how—by niching his agency's work and increasing his team's productivity—he could actually work with *fewer* clients to bring in *more* revenue.

By narrowing his agency's vertical specialization, Chris was able to strategically phase out clients that weren't the right fit, which in turn allowed his team to improve their processes and profitability. I also worked with him to improve his organizational structure and put the right people in the right positions, allowing his team to work more effectively.

Rankings.io now operates as a premium agency, with a select roster of larger-budget clients. Chris confidently quintupled his minimum pricing. And the changes paid off.

Altogether, Chris more sextupled his revenue (from $2MM to $12MM) in just four years. This growth has created security for his family, his team, and his clients. And he turned it into a book, to help other business owners: *Niching Up: The Narrower the Market, the Bigger the Prize.*

Five tips to increase team productivity

Want results like the ones Chris saw? There are many ways to increase your team's productivity. Begin with these five tips:

1. **Start measuring billables.** I recognize that no one enjoys time tracking. The good news? If your net profit margins are already 20-30%, you can skip tracking time (unless you bill Time & Materials). But if your net margins are below 20%, you *probably* have some profit leaks. You might need to do a month or two of time tracking to figure out where it's going. Measuring billables includes telling people their per-role billable targets. If you don't tell people, you can't expect them to read your mind.

2. **Get buy-in from job candidates on billable targets *before* you make an offer.** When hiring billable employees, tell them their billable target early. Their billable target at their previous agency might have been much lower than what you're expecting... or much higher. Make sure you're both on the same page, so you don't have any surprises. You can also create a new-hire ramp-up plan to make sure they're on track.

3. **Evaluate new client productivity impacts.** You also want to assess new clients—what are the productivity impacts to your team to work with them? Can you, for instance, assign work to existing team members? Great! That means generating more revenue without having to hire more people. On the other hand, is your team overloaded? Do you need to hire new team members? Consider what that means for future revenue, including the time and labor costs associated with onboarding.

4. **Require manager sign-off to waive billing.** Sometimes you'll do work where you *don't* bill the client. This can happen for many reasons, such as an error on the agency's part, or as a way to satisfy an unhappy client. You can define tiers for that (e.g., the project manager makes the call if it's under a certain amount; the director decides for the next tier; etc.) The key is that people need to get permission to waive billing a client. In my work as a project manager at a Time & Materials agency, I reviewed the time tracker every week to fix mis-coded entries.

5. **Dig into fixing other time leaks.** There may be other reasons why all of your team's time isn't billed. For instance, when people log their time just once a week—odds are, they're going to miss things. Missing 10-15 minutes in one day isn't a huge deal, but missing this a dozen times a week over the course of a year? That adds up to a *lot* of unbilled time. And that hurts your productivity.

If you want to grow revenue, you've probably considered hiring more people. That may be a good idea. But that's not the only way. **Consider per-capita revenue, too.**

KPI: Grow Your Per-Capita Revenue, Instead of Raw Revenue Alone

If you're not sure what your revenue *should* be, it's time to start comparing your agency's performance against industry benchmarks.

Don't love tracking metrics? You're not alone! Fortunately, just one number quickly conveys if you're *generally* on track: **"Rev/FTE"** (revenue per full-time equivalent), also known as "per-capita billables."

Rev/FTE is your agency's average annual services revenue per full-time equivalent team member. This is different from each person's billable target because Rev/FTE is an agency-wide annual average. Importantly, it excludes cost of goods sold (CoGS) and other pass-through items— including marked-up media buys, printing, and project-based contractors. Why? Because those aren't directly tied to the number of your primary team members.

Rev/FTE provides a consistent way to track productivity over time, even as your team and services change. Using this Rev/FTE figure, you'll be able to compare your agency to industry benchmarks and determine which levers will improve your future performance.

Does Rev/FTE explain *everything*? Nope, but it's a good place to start.

Using this Key Performance Indicator (KPI) to track progress can seem complicated at first, so I'm breaking it down into three steps for you.

Step 1: Calculate Rev/FTE

In short, Rev/FTE is your annual services revenue divided by your team headcount. Here's the formula:

(Services Revenue) / (FTE Count) = Rev/FTE

For the revenue, exclude things like commissions on pass-through expenses—because we're focusing on billable productivity relative to your headcount. For the FTE count, include owners, full-time employees, part-time employees, and any contractors who are doing work every week.

For now, let's consider a simple example. You have $5 million in total revenue, of which $200,000 is pass-through revenue for printing and media. Thus, your net revenue is $4.8 million. You have 18 full-time employees, 3 part-time employees (each working half-time), and several ongoing freelancers whose work totals 40 hours a week.

You'd take $4.8 million, divide by 20.5 FTE, and get $234K in Rev/FTE.

Is that any good? To answer that, let's look at the benchmarks.

Step 2: Compare your agency to industry benchmarks

Each agency is unique—but I've identified core industry benchmarks for Rev/FTE. Specialist agencies should have a higher Rev/FTE compared to generalist agencies because specialists should be charging premium prices.

◊ If you're a **generalist agency**, your annual Rev/FTE should be **$180,000 or higher**.

◊ If you're a **specialist agency**, your annual Rev/FTE should be **$250,000 or higher**.

Note: These figures apply as of 2023. If you're reading this in the distant future, be sure to adjust upward for inflation.

What if you're above or below the benchmark?

◊ If your Rev/FTE is above either number, you're doing well. And if it's approaching $300,000 or higher, you're doing really well.

◊ If your Rev/FTE is below $120,000, your agency is at risk of going out of business because there's minimal room for profits after you pay your team. (One exception: If all or most of your team is in a country with a very low cost of living.)

It's important to recalculate your Rev/FTE each year (or more often). Ask yourself, "Is my Rev/FTE going up, going down, or a mix?" Ideally it's going up over time due to premium pricing and keeping up with inflation.

If your Rev/FTE isn't meeting or above the benchmark (or you wish it were higher), there are a couple of things you can do to improve it.

Step 3: Use levers to improve the numbers behind your Rev/FTE

There are just two levers to improve Rev/FTE:

1. Increase revenue without increasing your team, and/or

2. Decrease the size of your team while delivering the same level of revenue.

Why might you decrease the size of your team? That can make sense if several team members always bill below their individual targets; you might choose to replace them with a more-productive team member.

Hiring and team management practices are key to improving your Rev/FTE. The following points will help get you there:

◊ As you grow revenue, don't hire immediately; try to generate revenue with your existing team.

◊ Don't immediately jump to hire a salesperson (or multiple salespeople) because they will increase the FTE count without immediately generating revenue... which means your Rev/FTE goes down (at least initially).

◊ Think strategically about hiring. Sometimes a moderately billable team member (e.g., a project manager or a team lead) is a good investment if they enable you to hire other team members who are highly billable.

◊ Don't tolerate low billable performance from a new team member, since they're hurting your services revenue in the future. This is a key reason to have a new-hire ramp-up plan (listing what you expect in week 1, month 1, month 2, etc.).

◊ If you hire ahead of demand, be sure your sales pipeline and employee onboarding process are ready to put people to work quickly.

Now it's your turn! Use the following exercise to apply this KPI as part of your "earn more" plan.

You may need to reach out to your accountant, operations head, or finance person to get the data. (And once you finalize the process, they can also do the calculations for you, both now and in the future.)

EXERCISE: Apply the Rev/FTE KPI at your agency. Record your answers here, in a doc on your computer or phone, or in the corresponding page of the companion workbook. Download your copy at WorkLessEarnMoreBook.com.

Let's look at your actual numbers. To summarize the steps:

1.   Gather your services revenue over the period.

2.   Gather your average FTE count over the period.

3.   To calculate your Rev/FTE, take services revenue and divide it by the average FTE count.

Likely, your Rev/FTE result will be somewhere between $100,000 and $400,000.

What's your Rev/FTE for the past 12 months? Record the answer here.

After calculating your agency's recent Rev/FTE, how far are you from the benchmark? *(Reminder: For a generalist agency, annual Rev/FTE is ideally $180,000 or higher; if you're running a specialist agency, your annual Rev/FTE is ideally $250,000 or higher.)*

Which lever(s) might you pull at *your* agency to improve your performance? Increase revenue from the current team? And/or reduce the size of your team? What are your next steps for this? (You'll see more growth ideas in Chapter 7.)

Bonus: Set revenue goals for a less-stressful year

How does your recent Rev/FTE compare to my industry benchmarks? Either way, it makes sense to set some goals for where you'd *like* to be, to start planning how you'll get there.

Setting revenue goals helps you be proactive, rather than reactive. By taking time to plan for the expected, you'll have time to improvise for the unexpected—and it won't be an emergency. (Or you'll have *fewer* emergencies, at least.)

There are many benefits to setting revenue goals. There are three categories of revenue goals:

◊ **Capacity Planning** to hire at the right time, upgrade your agency structure, and upgrade your internal processes before you hit crisis mode.

◊ **Runway and Compensation Planning** to know what you can pay yourself and your team, and to build runway to avoid or reduce mid-year financial crises.

◊ **Growth Style Alignment** to ensure you're making intentional progress toward your long-term goals, whether it's to sell or to build a sustainable lifestyle from your business (read more about this in the Introduction).

Wish you could put your agency on auto-pilot? **Setting revenue goals—including a revenue plan with monthly and quarterly targets—is even more important as you automate things.** Part of the process includes setting up an "early warning" system, to notify you if something isn't off-track. After all, it's (usually) easier to solve a problem when you have three months rather than three minutes of lead time.

How to set revenue goals is beyond the scope of this book, but I share how-to tips at the SakasAndCompany.com blog.

Now that you have benchmarks and solutions to profitably increase your revenue, it's time to enlist your team. In the next chapter, we'll review how to get their help.

TL; DR
Chapter 5: Earn More

In a hurry? Here's what to know:

♦ Most owners of independent agencies with under 100 people should pay themselves $150,000 to $500,000 a year in salary, plus shareholder distributions and benefits.

♦ Want a raise? There are nine key factors in setting your salary: agency revenue, profit margins, owner count, cost of living, weekly workload, tax planning, personal preference, pipeline, and self-confidence.

♦ To ensure you're paying yourself enough, consider what you'd need to pay someone else to replace you.

♦ There are three options for increasing your income: pay yourself more via existing profit margins, grow your top-line revenue, and/or grow your margins via higher productivity.

♦ Increasing productivity is crucial to work less and earn more. Labor typically consumes 50-60% of your revenue. To increase productivity: start tracking billables, require manager signoff to waive billing, and dig into fixing other time leaks.

♦ Consider growing per-capita revenue, not just total revenue. Calculate your Rev/FTE (services revenue divided by FTE count) to track productivity over time, compare to industry benchmarks, and decide how you'll improve your future performance.

♦ Access all of the tools and exercises mentioned here in the free companion workbook. You can download it at **WorkLessEarnMoreBook.com**.

Chapter 6:
Enlist Your Team

Don't Work Solo: Get Your Team's Help

Enlisting your team is arguably the most important piece of work less, earn more—after all, **you can't work less without others taking on some of your workload.** But effective delegation takes preparation and practice, and initially takes *more* work to bring team members up to speed.

Let's dig into how to make it feel less like "work" and more like "getting your time back."

Feeling Stuck? Here's How to Get Moving... Even When You're Too Busy to Delegate

What happens when your team misses deadlines or isn't meeting your quality standards? Or if *you're* the one struggling to get things done, as the overloaded agency owner? How do you get unstuck, especially if you feel too busy to delegate?

To run a successful agency, you can't just power through tasks to get them *done*—you need to do them *well*. And on time. And ideally not all done by you personally.

Fortunately, you don't have to guess at the solution! In my coaching, I've identified three dimensions to troubleshoot a not-done situation: **Desire, Competence, and Capacity (DCC).**

When you're missing *any* of these three things, you won't get things done *well*... and your agency (and profit margins) will suffer. **Once you use the model to identify the gaps, you can now take steps to fill those in.** And once you fill the gaps, you and your team will start getting things done.

Framework: Three requirements to get things done

When something important isn't happening at your agency, it's often because you don't have all three key points:

√   **Desire** (Do you WANT to do it?)

√   **Competence** (Do you know HOW to do it?)

√   **Capacity** (Do you have TIME to do it?)

Note: If you follow EOS, they brand their version (in a different order) as "GWC"—that is, "Get it, want it, capacity to get it done." Each approach is useful; choose the one that works best for you.

Here's a visual of Desire, Competence, and Capacity (DCC):

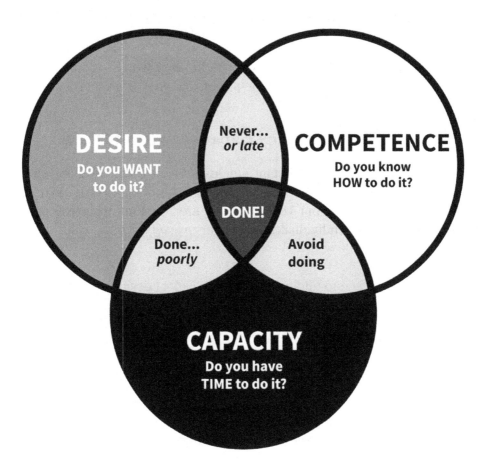

You can use my DCC model to troubleshoot (and then fix) things.

Let's review what happens when these misalign at agencies... and what happens they all three align.

Three mismatches... and just one match

There are several ways to go wrong and just one way to go right. To help you troubleshoot, let's look at the four combinations.

First, we'll look at why three combinations *don't* work... and then look at the winning combination that helps you and your team succeed.

Failure #1: Competence + Capacity, but not Desire

This is what I call the "reluctant employee"—they *can* do it and they have *time* to do it, but they *choose* to not do it. It's not always a *conscious* choice on their part—but you ultimately aren't getting what you need from them. (If the individual is an owner or executive, I'd call them a "reluctant leader.")

The solution? Dig into understanding their lack of desire.

◊ If it's not part of their core job, consider reassigning the task to someone else on the team.

◊ If it *is* part of their core job, that's a problem. For instance, this might be an account manager who doesn't like clients, or a project manager who doesn't like details.

If an employee lacks the desire to do a core part of their job, they need to be in a different job—whether at your agency or somewhere else.

And if *you're* the one lacking desire, assign things to someone else. (With some exceptions—you shouldn't delegate long-term vision or setting the culture, and you still need to manage your direct reports.)

Failure #2: Desire + Capacity, but not Competence

When someone has desire and capacity but not competence, it's a dangerous combination. Why? Because things usually get *done*, but they're done *poorly*. And without oversight, you may not notice the quality problem until it's too late.

Note that adding more oversight isn't a solution here—it's more work for everyone if one person always does a bad job.

You can address this via a combination of candidate screening, employee onboarding, and quality control. You—or your middle managers—need to keep an eye on things, rather than assume.

For instance, here's how I delegated my email newsletter to a new team member several years ago. The marketing automation process is not necessarily hard, but it's complex—and a mistake would reflect poorly on my brand.

◊ To train them, I recorded a screen-share on how to do it, after an intro about the goals and nuances.

◊ They then created written documentation, which didn't exist before.

◊ I asked them to record a screen-share as they scheduled the email in the queue, so I could review.

◊ I reviewed the screen-share video and saw that everything was on track—so I gave them the approval to proceed for future weeks.

◊ As a bonus, I've been able to re-use versions of this training documentation as my team onboards future people.

Failure #3: Desire + Competence, but not Capacity

This combo tends to happen to agency owners and leaders. That is, you *want* to do it and you *can* do it but you lack the *time* to get it done. And thus, your to-do list grows.

Sometimes the solution is a matter of resetting how you spend your time. Other times, it's enlisting others to help with some or all of the work. Or it's creating heads-down time in your schedule when people know not to interrupt you.

In coaching, I help agency owners set monthly goals that contribute to their long-term goals. This helps them focus, which helps them get things done.

Want to kick it up a notch? My goal-setting process also includes clients setting a reward and a consequence. This gamification gives people an extra nudge, because it's a reward and a consequence *they* chose.

Success: Desire + Competence + Capacity (DCC)

Here's where it all aligns! When you (or a team member) have desire and competence and capacity, things tend to get done, and they get done well.

If you're struggling—or you see one of your direct reports struggling— try using the DCC model to troubleshoot the situation.

Using my three-factor model also **helps you reduce the sense of blame**. If someone isn't doing something, it's usually *not* that they're a terrible person—they're just missing 1-2 key factors. If they're willing to address those, you can move forward together.

Think about areas where *you're* struggling to get things done. Is it primarily because you're missing desire, competence, or capacity? Use the exercise below to troubleshoot. In the following section, we'll look at how to address these.

EXERCISE: Reflect on the following questions. Record your answers here, in a doc on your computer or phone, or in the corresponding page of the workbook. Download your copy at WorkLessEarnMoreBook.com.

What are some tasks that you've assigned to yourself (or have defaulted to you, as the agency leader) that aren't getting done?

Now, dig into *why* they aren't getting done—based on what's missing from the DCC model. (A task may appear in more than one category.)

List the tasks where the doer is missing **desire:**

List the tasks where the doer is missing **competence:**

List the tasks where the doer is missing **capacity:**

Now, based on what you've observed: **What might you do to close the gap(s)?**

As a bonus, repeat the DCC exercise by focusing on a task or responsibility that one of your *employees* isn't completing. Use the three-part model to dig into which part (or parts) are missing.

Next, let's explore what you might do to close the gap(s).

Work Less, Earn More

Start Getting Things Off Your Plate: D/D/D/D

Once you understand *why* things aren't getting done, it's time to make them happen. The solution? Get things off your plate.

If you want to work less, you'll need to shift how you approach your to-do list.

◊   Sometimes that means you don't do something at all.

◊   Other times, you'll hand a to-do to someone else.

◊   And other times, you complete it yourself... but later.

◊   Ideally, the only to-do items remaining are the ones that are most important for you to do now.

There's a simple way to think about this. As a shortcut, I think of it as **Do/Drop/Delegate/Defer** (aka "D/D/D/D"). Any task can fit into one of those four categories:

◊   **Do:** It's something you *absolutely* have to handle yourself and that needs to be done now. It'll stay on your calendar or to-do list. Ideally, these are mostly "$1,000-an-hour tasks"—the things only you can do.

◊   **Drop:** Delete it from your to-do list... and *don't* assign it to anyone else. (Note: If someone is relying on you to do it, let them know that it's not happening.)

◊   **Delegate:** Assign it to someone else on your team (but be sure you use S.M.A.R.T. goals so they're clear on what "done" looks like).

◊   **Defer:** You'll do it... later. ("Later" could be tomorrow, later this week, next month, or another future point.)

Review your to-do list. What are some things you might be able to D/D/D/D?

If you find yourself struggling with this, you're not alone! Many agency owners have a hard time letting go. Every item on their to-do list seems to be both **urgent** and **important**. That is, it needs to be done *quickly* and by the person they trust most to do it *well*. In the early days of an agency, owners tend to assign that work to... themselves.

Because of this, **delegation** is tough: It's the D/D/D/D option most of my clients struggle to accept as part of their role as an agency owner.

If this rings true for you, consider: How urgent or important is each of the tasks on your to-do list? If something isn't actually *that* urgent, could you take the time to teach someone else how to do it? If something isn't actually that important, could you hand it off with clear instructions (and some level of oversight)?

Investing in your team members' ability to do these tasks now means they can take them off your plate in the future.

Sidebar: Why is delegating so hard?

If you break it down, **delegation is more complicated than you might expect.** From my analysis, it involves at least 15 steps—from recognizing that you should delegate, to hiring someone to do the work, to creating a plan to re-integrate the results into your own workflow. Fortunately, it gets easier with practice, and you don't have to do all 15 steps *every* time.

Once you have a concrete list of things to delegate, it becomes a lot easier to imagine assigning those tasks to someone else. There's a psychological step you need to take here—you need to accept that your job is to get results through other people.

That is, your job has shifted from **Technician** to **Manager** and **Entrepreneur.** (For more on the concept and the continuum, see Michael Gerber's *The E-Myth Revisited*.) Delegating is actually about growth—for you and your team. You've learned how to do the tasks you're going to delegate; the next step is to teach someone else how to do them so that you can move on to doing higher-value work. But this means you have to be ready to let go of doing it all yourself.

Remember: when done well, delegation is a win-win. You provide someone else on your team an opportunity to grow and develop their own skills and gain extra time in your own schedule so that you can do a better job at the things you decided you needed to handle yourself.

Delegation helps you step away from work

Consider serial entrepreneur **Mike King**, the founder of award-winning SEO agency **iPullRank**. He found delegation to be key to both the success of his agency *and* his ability to prioritize personal goals.

He reached out when he realized that executive coaching could help create the structure he needed to stay on track with his big ideas, both in and outside the agency. In our work, I encouraged him to hire a fractional CFO and a head of operations to help him reach his long-term financial goals.

Three years after our coaching relationship began, iPullRank had tripled its revenue. Additionally, helping Mike spread responsibilities across his team allowed him to prepare for the birth of his second daughter—creating the space to *finally* take family leave. All of this happened thanks to delegation.

Three shortcuts to improve your delegation

Delegation is complex, and managers who don't do it well end up with frustrated teams—employees either don't have the information they need to do the job or they become victims of micromanaging. Neither scenario is good for you or your agency. So, how do you keep this from happening to you?

Once you're ready to delegate, it helps to understand how to do it *well*. Here are some tools you can use to manage efficient and happy teams.

Shortcut #1: Use S.M.A.R.T. goals

When you assign tasks to your team, be sure they understand what's expected of them by using S.M.A.R.T. goals.

Ultimately, S.M.A.R.T. goals help clarify what "done" really means. For a refresher on the concept, go back to Chapter 4.

Shortcut #2: Get clear on Swim Lanes, via A.R.C.I.

Keep people on task with **Swim Lanes** (more on that in Chapter 2). And use an A.R.C.I. matrix (also known as a R.A.C.I. matrix) to reduce confusion. That is, clarify who is:

◊ **Accountable:** Who owns that the work happens? They're on the hook, even if they're not the responsible doer. As the owner, you're ultimately accountable for anything that happens at the business.

◊ **Responsible:** Who does the actual hands-on work?

◊ **Consulted:** Who needs to give feedback to the responsible person as things get done?

◊ **Informed:** Who needs to be kept in the loop? Importantly, this person does not have *input* on things; they just need to be aware of what's happening, even if they're notified after the task is complete.

Are you running into team or client drama? Consider taking time to define A.R.C.I. roles. For example, if someone is Informed but *thinks* they should be Consulted, they'll be unhappy that you "ignored" them. Or if someone doesn't realize they're responsible for a project... it won't end well.

Make sure that everyone involved on a project knows their role is by completing an A.R.C.I. matrix at kickoff. You'll find a sample A.R.C.I. matrix in the companion workbook, which you can customize to your specific team.

Shortcut #3: Pre-schedule interim check-ins

How do you help keep your team accountable without becoming a micromanager? Use pre-scheduled check-ins!

Say you assign someone to do a task that you believe will take them two weeks to complete—but they've never done this task before (or never done it for *you*). You might pre-schedule two check-ins:

◊ Schedule one check-in **at 10-20% of the timeline** to see how it's going. Have they run into any snags, or do they need access to something they don't have? An early check-in will help head off any potential problems or highlight resources or information the assignee didn't initially realize they needed.

◊ Schedule one check-in **at 50-60% of the timeline** to see how things are progressing. That way, if anything's off-track, you have time to get it back on track *before* the deadline.

◊ Of course, you'll also check-in **at the end of the project** to review the work and how things went.

On a longer project, you might schedule more check-ins. And you might also split the project into smaller chunks overall, with a more in-depth review after each milestone.

You may have noticed: these are all examples of improving your communication skills. As a former boss liked to say, miscommunications happen because we are "separated by a common language." That is, you think you're on the same page... but that may not be true.

Want to improve how you communicate? Read on for some bonus tips!

Bonus: Tips on being a better communicator

If you want to get better at delegating, you'll want to improve your communication skills. After all, it's not just about *what* you say. Communicating is only effective if the other person understands what you're saying in the way that you intended.

With that in mind, here are some tips for becoming a better communicator:

◊ **Include details.** Want to ensure that your expectations are met? Communicate what you're looking for with as much detail as possible. Details can include timelines, specific deliverables, names of people to collaborate with, deadlines, expectations for quality, etc. Your team can't read your mind.

◊ **Put it in writing.** Keep everyone on the same page by outlining project tasks in writing, either while you're going through a meeting or after you delegate something. If you're having a meeting related to a project—no matter how big or small—keep a running notes document that everyone has access to. Use the document (or a version in your PM system) to track action items with due dates and who is responsible for each. Team members can refer back to it if they have questions, and if something *doesn't* get done, the document can show where the breakdown happened.

◊ **Be ready to provide support.** It's great when you have team members you can just hand off work to—essentially set it and forget it until the task is completed. But in general, you should anticipate receiving follow-up questions after you've delegated work. Use pre-scheduled interim check-ins to offer up support to team members who might not feel comfortable asking for help— or who don't realize they need it!

◊ **Give credit where credit is due.** Recognize and thank everyone who was involved. After all, you're all working together to accomplish these goals, and everyone values being recognized for their hard work. Remember: **As a leader, your team's success is *your* success**.

What to delegate as an agency owner—and in what order

Not sure what you can take off your plate? Here's the order I'd recommend for delegating different areas of your work as your agency grows:

◊ **Eliminate subject matter expert work from your responsibilities first.** As you transition into the role of a manager, you move away from being a subject matter expert (and that's okay—you have other responsibilities now!). This involves any work that could be done by a designer, developer, copywriter, analyst, specialist, or QA technician. This work is generally invisible to your clients so they won't necessarily know you're not doing it. Often, this can be delegated to freelancers.

◊ **Then, delegate project management.** This work tends to be more internal; again, clients won't necessarily know that you've handed this off. However, you might choose to continue on as the client-facing account manager at this stage.

◊ **The next step is to delegate account management.** Assign someone from your team as the day-to-day contact while you come in to do high-level client strategy.

◊ **You may choose to delegate business development early, if you don't like sales.** Or you might choose to *close* deals while delegating early-stage sales to other members of your team.

◊ **Client strategy is one of the last areas to delegate.** Once you've successfully delegated other aspects of your work, you'll have more capacity to provide oversight for handing off client strategy, which can be harder to navigate than other areas.

Ultimately, you get to choose what you do. If you want to do some lower-level work, that's your choice—but be sure it *feels* like a choice, rather than an obligation.

Example: D/D/D/D during the hiring process

Now that you understand *how* and *what* to delegate to your team, let's look at an example. Imagine you're in the midst of hiring, and you're feeling overwhelmed about the hiring process on top of your regular work.

As an agency owner, hiring is an important part of your job. If a new hire reports to you, you need to talk to the finalist candidates, do the reference checks, and so on. But as you grow, you can delegate *aspects* of hiring.

With that in mind, here are some things about hiring that could go into each D/D/D/D category:

◊ **Do**: Do the final reference check calls; since the person reports to you, you want to hear the answers directly.

◊ **Drop**: Stop creating unnecessary new procedures for hiring—don't reinvent the wheel! Use what's worked in the past, or pull from the many resources that already exist. Also, eliminate extra rounds of interviews; focus on what's most important, rather than having them talk to every single future coworker.

◊ **Delegate**: Assign a qualified colleague to pre-screen resumes before they get to you. You'll invest time to "train" them on your preferred criteria, and can adjust as you go.

◊ **Defer**: Delay the next round of interviews to next week while you handle certain crises this week. Be sure you (or a colleague) communicate to candidates about the delay, so you don't leave them wondering.

What if you don't have enough help?

What if you don't *have* someone to delegate to? In that case, it might be time to expand your agency's capacity by hiring it out—through outside contractors or full- or part-time staff. It gets easier to delegate as you grow, since you have more help.

If you're not in a place where you can expand capacity, it unfortunately means you'll have to keep doing what you're currently doing (for now). But it's not forever. Instead, explore the tools in the next couple of chapters on strategizing for growth. Once you're ready to expand your team, you'll already have the tools you need to be a better delegator.

Now that we've reviewed the basics, we'll create a "choose your own adventure" plan to work less and earn more. Coming up in Chapter 7, I'll share options to help agencies like yours.

TL; DR
Chapter 6: Enlist Your Team
In a hurry? Here's what to know:

- Delegation takes preparation and practice. Use my desire, competence, and capacity (DCC) framework to troubleshoot and then fix problems.
- If you want to work less, you need to shift how you approach your to-do list. Use Do/Drop/Delegate/Defer (D/D/D/D) to get things off your plate.
- There are three shortcuts you can use to become a better delegator: use S.M.A.R.T. goals, clarify roles via swim lanes and an A.R.C.I. matrix, and pre-schedule interim check-ins.
- Not sure what to delegate first? Consider delegating in this order: 1) subject matter expert, 2) project management, 3) account management, 4) business development, and 5) client strategy.
- If you don't have enough people on board to delegate to—and can't currently expand your agency's capacity—explore the tools in the next chapters on strategizing for growth. Then, come back to this chapter when you're ready to start delegating.
- Access all of the tools and exercises mentioned here in the free companion workbook. You can download it at **WorkLessEarnMoreBook.com**.

Chapter 7:

Strategies and Tactics to Grow Your Agency

Use These to Build Your Work Less, Earn More Plan

Enlisting your team is important... but how do you let them know where you're going? Start by choosing a strategy, then pick the tactics that'll make it happen.

Sidebar: Strategy vs. Tactic?

It's not always clear: what's a "strategy" versus a "tactic"?

For most businesses, a strategy is a combination of decisions to accomplish a specific goal, and tactics are smaller actions that contribute to fulfilling the strategy.

For our purposes: You'll choose two of the 25 tactics, and that pair of two tactics will be the strategy behind how you'll approach work less, earn more in the coming 90 days. And then you can adjust over time.

Yes, a strategy is usually more complicated than picking two tactics to follow. But don't get in your own way; the point is to make a decision for the next 90 days and then adjust from there.

Stop procrastinating! Create forward motion; action begets action.

Five Agency Growth Themes

Your strategic choices are the foundation of your 90-day implementation plan—which we'll get to in the next chapter. You'll also get free access to my 90-day plan template in the companion workbook.

In working with agency owners, I've found that the most common high-impact tactics can be divided into five themes:

1. **Delivery optimization**: Deliver current work more profitably to increase profit margins.

2. **Marketing and sales optimization:** Improve lead-gen and sales process to grow top-line revenue.

3. **Leadership and Management**: Level-up as a manager to accomplish more via your team.

4. **Service optimization:** Shift the services you offer to deliver work more profitably.

5. **Specialized positioning**: Focus on client industry vertical(s) to charge more via premium pricing.

Each of these themes includes multiple tactics—a total of 25 altogether, ranging from firing your worst clients to changing your team structure. **You don't need to complete all 25 of these to reach your goals.** Your 90-day implementation plan will be focused on the two most important tactics for *your* agency. **That duo is your "Work Less, Earn More" strategy for the next three months.**

Consider, for example, **Nicolas Jacobeus**—the founder of custom software development agency **Belighted**. After leading his agency for more than a decade, he'd grown tired of the long process to sell custom work and had lost enthusiasm.

Nicolas wanted the flexibility to travel and to pursue new business opportunities—but he was integral to the sales process and to client escalation. To achieve his long-term goals, he needed to optimize his team and build recurring revenue so he could delegate more work. As his business coach, I helped lay the groundwork for him to become fully optional at his agency by focusing on two main tactics:

1. Changing team structure, and

2. Hiring a strong second-in-command.

When COVID-19 hit, Nicolas found himself stuck in Bali. His two-week trip turned into four months away from his team. The separation accelerated implementing his "Work Less, Earn More" plan.

Thanks to our previous conversations, he was able to move forward. He also sped up hiring a CEO to manage day-to-day operations—and Nicolas is now involved just a few hours a month as chairman.

Ready to become more (or fully) optional at *your* agency? Let's look at the full list of tactics you can implement into your work less, earn more plan.

The Full List: 25 Tactics to Grow Your Agency

This is a basic guide to my 25 tactics for agency growth. Many of these require additional information to implement *well*—luckily, you can find more information about these on the blog at SakasAndCompany.com.

IMPORTANT: As you read through these tactics, keep a running list of which 3-5 seem most appealing. That'll make choosing your top two (in the next chapter) easier, as they will become the basis of your 90-day plan.

THEME #1: Delivery Optimization

These tactics help you deliver current work more profitably.

A. Improve team productivity

→ Review team structure and workflow to identify and eliminate overlaps and inefficiencies.

→ Research and evaluate PM tools to improve workflow.

→ Evaluate team members' skills to ensure everyone is in the right role.

→ Re-read Chapter 3 for a refresher on structuring roles.

→ Re-read about "Rev/FTE" (per-capita billables) in Chapter 5.

B. Stop over-delivering to clients

→ Identify and eliminate scope creep at your agency.

→ Improve your estimates and clarify your Statements of Work (SOWs).

→ Use my "Reason-Options-Choose" (R-O-C) negotiation framework to say "no" without directly saying "no":

  • Cite a **Reason** why you can't do what they want.

  • Give them two-to-three **Options** that you'd be comfortable with.

  • Let them **Choose** which they prefer.

→ Create guidelines and a clear escalation path for team members on handling client demands (e.g., asking clients, "Would you like an estimate for that?" for requests outside of project scope).

C. Fire your worst clients

→ Identify if you have a 'client dilution' problem (e.g., small-budget clients demanding big-budget service from your agency). And then identify why, so you can start reducing your client count without hurting the business.

→ Rank your best and worst clients... and then fire the bad ones.

→ Commit to firing any toxic clients before they create (more) staff turnover.

→ Use my "Strategic Churn" concept—replacing bad, mediocre, or low-paying clients with higher-paying great clients—to organize the client-firing process, if your sales funnel is strong enough to support the intentional churn.

D. Revamp how you deliver your current services

→ Do a work breakout (WBO)—a quantitative debrief that evaluates how much work it took your team to complete a project or retainer—to identify delivery-related profit leaks.

→ Nail down the agency roles you're using to deliver services. (See Chapter 3 for my guide to agency roles.)

→ Shift how you assign and manage work, including defining swim lanes. (See the Introduction for a refresher on swim lanes.)

→ Re-read the values, goals, and resources (VGR) section in Chapter 2—then clarify and communicate those to your team. And consider how to share with every future hire, too.

THEME #2: Marketing and Sales Optimization

These tactics help you to improve lead-gen and sales process.

E. Grow your marketing funnel and your sales funnel

→ Focus on the right marketing priorities, especially if you're delegating (aspects of) marketing tasks to your team.

→ Build your sales funnel.

→ If and when you need to hire, hire the *right* level of marketer. Sometimes, they might be freelancers.

F. Improve sales process

→ Pre-qualify your agency's sales prospects with a questionnaire to better understand them—*before* they become a client.

→ Clarify big questions via email so you've documented the answers.

→ Validate prospects against B.A.N.T. (Budget, Authority, Need, Timing), C.R.U.X. (Compatible, Realistic, Urgent, X-Factor), or another qualifying checklist.

→ Do an exploratory call before dedicating time to creating a sales proposal.

→ Pre-schedule a proposal-review meeting (or video call), rather than just emailing clients a proposal.

→ Use client onboarding to set expectations and clarify scope. The salesperson attends the kickoff, but the account manager leads the onboarding process.

G. Hire a full-stack salesperson

→ Define the role, incentives, and comp plan.

→ Review how hiring a new salesperson will impact your profits, PM process, and agency workload.

→ Ask the right sales interview questions. The key is to focus on values and behaviors that match what you need in the sales role.

→ Hold them accountable for results. They need time to ramp-up... but they don't have forever to produce.

H. Chunk-out lower-level sales tasks

→ Map the steps of your current sales process.

→ Identify what a lower-skilled person could do (e.g., acknowledging initial sales inquiries, asking prospects to complete a pre-questionnaire, doing an initial introductory or exploratory call to qualify the prospect, and/or scheduling a 1:1 follow-up call with you as the experienced salesperson).

→ Assign a high-potential current team member to help you screen sales prospects before you speak with prospects as the closer.

I. Increase your prices

→ Understand the three pricing models for agencies: hourly, milestone, and value-based.

→ Use value-anchoring to charge more with new clients. That is, consider the potential impact your clients are likely to see and price your work as a fraction of that likely-high return.

→ Raise prices for current clients—I recommend a portfolio approach, where you adjust the increase to reflect each client's circumstances. That is, rank your clients and group them by those that will receive a larger vs. smaller price increase.

→ Consider repositioning as a strategy-first agency to help you justify higher prices.

J. Increase recurring revenue

→ Think strategically about retainers, including the pros and cons.

→ Consider how to profitably handle maintenance and support requests—whether internally or referring it out.

→ Incorporate recurring revenue into your sales process, including initial paid discovery projects to help you scope retainer-based follow-on work.

THEME #3: Leadership and Management

These tactics help you level-up as a manager.

K. Commit to better delegation

→ Understand why delegation is hard—and what to do about it (read more on this in Chapter 6).

→ Ward off burnout by putting your own oxygen mask on first (e.g., take some mental health days!).

→ Commit to (increasingly) eliminate client-facing work—starting with subject matter expert (SME) work, and then project management, and then account management.

→ When you feel overwhelmed, take 15 minutes to recharge away from work (and then get help fixing the underlying problems).

L. Recruit, onboard, and manage a strong assistant

→ Understand the importance of doing "$1,000 an hour" activities. That is, what are the things that only *you* can do as the agency owner (hypothetically worth $1,000 an hour) versus something that a lower-paid team member could do?

→ Get clear on what to expect from an executive assistant (EA)... and what they should expect from you.

→ Consider what you can delegate to a virtual assistant (VA)—more on this in Chapter 10.

M. Build and coach a layer of middle managers

→ Dig into whether a person eligible for a promotion towards management truly understands what the job title entails.

→ If your middle managers are doing too much client-facing work, consider hiring freelancers to help.

→ Read my book *Made to Lead: A Pocket Guide to Managing Marketing & Creative Teams*, available on Amazon. (It's a quick, helpful, 30-minute read.; most people report reading it in less than 30 minutes.)

N. Hire, onboard, and coach a strong second-in-command (2iC)

→ Consider succession planning, ideally as a promotion from within. (But make sure they know what they're getting into.)

→ Read *Riding Shotgun: The Role of the COO* by Nate Bennett and Stephen Miles, for insights on the bespoke COO role.

→ If you need to hire externally, be clear on the role you need them to fulfill... including their specific new-hire ramp-up plan.

→ Create incentive alignment, including tools like phantom stock.

→ Consider a framework like David Skok and Josh Hannah's "Extreme Referencing." That is, go beyond a cursory reference check; dig deeper and ask tough questions.

→ If you're struggling to decide between two finalists, use my "Make Hard Decisions" framework:

   o Identify potential directions to explore.

   o Narrow things down to 2-3 options.

   o Write one Advance Retrospective for each of the options (get a refresher on this in Chapter 1).

   o Reflect on which feels best. Do you "know" now?

   o Draft a v0 ("version zero") plan to onboard each person.

O. Recruit outside help (e.g., therapist, coach, fractional CFO)

→ Get clear on whether you need someone to share advice (e.g., consultant or consultant-style coach), help you find your own answers from within (e.g., coach or therapist), or roll up their sleeves to do the work (e.g., fractional CFO). Consider the personal advisor roles outlined in Chapter 3.

→ Seek recommendations from fellow agency owners, either 1:1 or via agency networks and communities.

→ Use my "Hiring Another Agency" steps to organize your selection and decision process, since both focus on hiring professional services. You can find this article at SakasAndCompany.com.

P. Develop your strengths, and hire to fill your weaknesses (and non-fun strengths)

→ Identify your strengths... and your weaknesses. And identify if there are strengths you don't *like* doing.

→ See Chapter 6 for advice on enlisting your team to start doing anything you're not great at (or don't like doing).

Q. Coach your middle managers on coaching their team

→ Read—and then assign them to read—my article on coaching your team. You can find this article, and more, on my blog at SakasAndCompany.com.

→ Assign them to subscribe to my "Become a Better Manager in 30 Days" email series (for a month of free daily tips). It's free via, yes, SakasAndCompany.com.

→ Do weekly one-on-one ("O3") meetings, to coach them on coaching their team. (You might need to meet more often if they're facing new issues.)

R. Hire a senior lead to level-up the team's productivity through coaching

→ *Note: This is similar to tactics N and Q—but here, I assume you don't have (a) middle manager(s) yet.*

→ Start by reviewing your current team for promotion-from-within opportunities. Remember, "good at their specialty" doesn't *automatically* mean "good at managing people in that specialty." This may include creating a professional development plan to help employees grow into future roles.

→ If you need to hire externally, be clear on the role you need them to do; don't hire a reluctant manager, or someone who's over- or under-qualified for your budget and your needs.

→ Consider using a dialed-back version of Extreme Referencing (from tactic N).

S. Change your team structure to level-up your ability to generate revenue

→ Be strategic about the agency roles you're using (more on agency roles in Chapter 3).

→ Identify "breakpoints" to shift your team structure as you grow your headcount.

→ Eliminate yourself as a day-to-day contact for your agency's clients, since you don't scale.

THEME #4: Service Optimization

These tactics help you shift the services you offer.

T. Eliminate your outdated services

→ Debrief with your sales team on which services tend to get the most (downward) pricing pressure from prospects, as well as any services that no longer meet a market demand.

→ Do a work breakout (WBO) exercise to see which services are least profitable (or even unprofitable).

→ Consider whether to keep *some* low-margin services, if they fulfill a more-strategic purpose (e.g., offering cross-sell services to retain large clients that primarily use other, more profitable services).

→ Before you eliminate any services, evaluate the financial impact of losing low-margin revenue that's subsidizing agency-wide overhead.

U. Expand your differentiator services

→ Review where your clients see you as indispensable.

→ Debrief with your team on which services are unique and high-margin, vs. generic and high-competition.

→ Consider how your services fit into three categories: Think (strategy), Teach (training and empowerment), or Do (implementation). Do your services fit together cohesively?

→ Look for opportunities to position your services as strategy-first.

V. Add new services

→ Read my in-depth article on adding new services on the blog at SakasAndCompany.com.

→ Weigh whether to staff new services from your current team, via new freelancers, through strategic partner agencies, and/or via new employee hires.

THEME #5: Specialized Positioning

These tactics help you focus on client industry verticals:

W. Commit to an industry-vertical specialization

→ Consider why it's important for most agencies to specialize: My specialist clients tend to be less-stressed and more profitable.

→ Choose the right client industry vertical based on what's lucrative now (and in the likely future), where you have experience (and can show results), and what you enjoy.

→ Accept that there's no perfect industry. There's no industry out there with enormous client budgets yet zero competition. Don't choose impulsively... but don't wait forever, either.

→ On the fence? Create marketing around a new vertical without making that the sole focus. If it takes off, you can make a bigger commitment to the client industry.

X. Clarify your unique selling proposition (USP) and differentiators

→ Sit down to reflect on what makes your agency unique compared to the competition. (I know, I know... it's easy to do this for your clients and hard to do it for yourself.)

→ Get input from others—your team, your current clients, your prospects. It's hard to make decisions in a vacuum, especially since you're so close to the subject.

→ Incorporate your takeaways into your marketing and sales efforts.

Y. Execute ongoing marketing to match the positioning

→ Does your marketing consistently reflect your current positioning? If not, it's time for some updates. Don't be an agency that's afraid to publicly declare your specialization—that defeats the purpose.

→ Now that you've specialized, it's time for thought leadership... and marketing automation. That is, share useful advice—and make it easy for people to opt-in to your marketing automation or other email lists.

→ If you want to do public speaking (whether virtually or in-person) and/or podcast guest appearances, check out my first book: *The In-Demand Marketing Agency: How to Use Public Speaking to Become an Agency of Choice*, available on Amazon. It's all about speaking for agency lead-gen. And don't forget to have an email opt-in process to get people on your list.

Take a deep breath; I know that list is a lot to take in. If you've done an initial skimming, step away for a bit, and then re-read it more closely.

Next Steps: Create a Shortlist of 3-5 Tactics

Now consider your future 3-5 tactic options from the list above.

EXERCISE: Reflect on the following questions. Record your answers here, in a doc on your computer or phone, or in the corresponding page of the workbook. Download your copy at WorkLessEarnMoreBook.com.

Which tactics appeal to you? Which align with pain points you've noticed at your agency? Record your top 3-5 tactics. You'll refer to these in the next chapter as you narrow your options.

Need help fine-tuning your favorite tactics? In the next chapter, I'll share methods for narrowing the list to two options that make sense *right now*, so you can focus on the best-fit options first.

TL; DR
Chapter 7: Strategies and Tactics to Grow

In a hurry? Here's what to know:

◆ Your strategic choices are the foundation of your 90-day implementation plan—and that strategy will be made up of several tactics that help make it happen.

◆ In working with agency owners, I've found that the most common high-impact tactics can be divided into five themes. Each of these themes includes multiple tactics—a total of 25 altogether:
   o Theme #1: Delivery optimization
   o Theme #2: Marketing and sales optimization
   o Theme #3: Leadership and management
   o Theme #4: Service optimization
   o Theme #5: Specialized positioning

◆ Consider 3-5 tactic options from the list of 25 (go back in the chapter for specific details) based on which ones appeal to you and which align with pain points you've noticed in your agency.

◆ In the next chapter, we'll talk about how to narrow down to your two best-fit options as the core of your 90-day plan.

◆ Access all of the tools and exercises mentioned here in the free companion workbook. You can download it at **WorkLessEarnMoreBook.com.**

Chapter 8:

Choose Your Growth Strategy

Choose Two Tactics as the Strategy Behind Your 90-Day Plan

From the last chapter, you've ideally created a shortlist of **3-5 growth tactic options**. Now, we'll narrow that shortlist to your top two tactics. Those two (one primary, one secondary) will be the strategy behind your 90-day plan. (As a reminder, you'll get a template for that 90-day plan in the next chapter.)

You may be overwhelmed by the sheer number of options... or maybe you're excited and want to implement a dozen tactics at once!

Whichever way you're feeling, note that **it's important to keep your focus on a maximum of two options for now.**

Remember S.M.A.R.T. goals from Chapter 4? Narrowing your focus will help you *reach* your goals—by choosing a realistic target for your "Work Less, Earn More" plan. You can always choose other tactics for future 90-day periods. When you focus, you're more likely to get results.

Consider **Joe Quinn**, the co-founder and CEO of agency **Big Vision**. As demand quickly outpaced what he and Alyse—his wife and co-founder—could fulfill, he was stuck in the weeds. Soon after starting their agency, they began hiring people to handle client fulfillment. Joe now found himself managing a team while also being involved in the day-to-day work. He was acting as agency owner, account manager, project manager, and more.

Wanting to work less and earn more, Joe reached out for my help. Seeing how much project-based work the agency was doing, I recommended Joe enlist his entire team to focus on **one** agency growth tactic: grow recurring revenue (that is, tactic "J" from the list in Chapter 7).

What did that look like? His marketing team began featuring case studies with recurring-revenue examples. His sales team highlighted ongoing solutions, rather than one-off projects. Delivery team members mentioned the benefits of retainers during initial projects. And account managers and project managers worked with clients to deliver value to improve renewals. Combined, these highly-focused shifts—centered around a single core tactic—helped Joe grow monthly recurring revenue (MRR) from 10% to 90% in about a year. And Joe can sleep better at night, knowing his agency's success no longer depends on his continuous day-to-day involvement.

How to Narrow Your List of Options to Two Tactics: Three Shortcuts

So, how do you narrow *your* options as I did with Joe? In my work as a coach, I've identified three decision-making shortcuts for agency owners. As you read through these, think about which matches how you prefer to make decisions. Then, use that framework to narrow your list to two options.

Decision shortcut #1: Logic-driven

If you're **logic-driven**, consider which tactics on your shortlist are either high impact or quick wins. You might choose one of each for your implementation plan.

Or, consider which tactics are urgent and which are important for *your* agency. As I mentioned in Chapter 6, not everything that's urgent is important, and vice versa. Consider using your 90-day implementation plan to make progress on things that are Important but not Urgent, since those otherwise tend to slip through the cracks.

Decision shortcut #2: Feelings-driven

If you're someone who goes with your gut when making decisions, you're probably more **feelings-driven** than logic-driven. In this case, take the options you've selected so far and put them in order of priority based on what you're feeling right now. What seems most important? What seems least important? Don't worry about getting it right—just make your list, **then sleep on it**.

When you look at it again the next day, does it still feel like the right list? If it does, congrats! You'll build your plan around the first two options you've written down (and for now, delete the rest). If the list *doesn't* feel right the next day, restructure it based on any new thoughts or gut feelings, and sleep on it again.

Remember: You're only choosing these for the next 90 days. You can change priorities or pick different combinations in the future. Don't take forever to decide—pick two tactics and move forward.

And if you're feeling *really* stuck...

Decision shortcut #3: Benchmark-driven

This shortcut is for people who can't quite narrow down the list of options—it's the **benchmark-driven** shortcut. Here, you'll look at what *other* people have chosen, and pick from those. But make sure you're picking tactics that make sense for *your* agency.

Through my coaching and bootcamps, I've found that most people will pick at least *one* of these eight tactics for their 90-day implementation plan. To help make your decision even easier, I've noted which are high impact, which are quick wins, and which fall into *both* categories. *Note that they're also tagged by the letters used in Chapter 7, so you can easily flip back to find more information on each one.*

High-impact tactics

C. **Fire your worst clients.** If you've got terrible clients, fire them. Bad clients don't help you grow—and certainly don't help you work less. In fact, terrible clients often *get in the way* of earning more.

Q. **Coach your middle managers.** To your frontline employees, your middle managers *are* the agency. Coaching your middle managers helps create an environment where team members can succeed... without your having to do all the work yourself.

Quick Wins tactics

K. **Commit to better delegation.** As I've mentioned before, delegation isn't just handing over a task and hoping it gets done. But it's not about micro-management, either. Good delegation means striking the right balance between trust and oversight.

T. **Eliminate outdated services.** These are services where your agency isn't a strong competitor or that no longer serve your needs. Remember: you don't *have* to offer every single service that anyone has ever asked you to provide.

Tactics for *both* high impact and quick wins

B. Stop over-delivering. Scope creep is an extremely common agency problem. Learning how to say "no"—or to charge more—helps you produce profitable work.

H. Chunk-out sales tasks. For instance, is there someone who could screen initial sales inquiries? As your agency grows, this is a task you can easily take off of your to-do list.

I. Increase your prices. Agency owners are often concerned about raising prices because of the risk of losing clients. But there are ways to mitigate this, such as by using the portfolio approach mentioned in Chapter 7.

X. Clarify your Unique Selling Proposition (USP). Note: this doesn't mean you should revamp your *entire* positioning (at least, not as a "quick" win). Instead, the tactic is about ensuring your website and other marketing materials align with what you're telling people in sales calls and emails.

Now it's time to narrow your shortlist to just two tactics! Use one of the shortcuts above to choose your top two growth tactics for your 90-day plan.

Note: Most people will choose two tactics. But if your primary choice is particularly complicated for your agency to implement, it's okay to choose just one.

<u>EXERCISE: Reflect on the following questions. Record your answers here, in a doc on your computer or phone, or in the corresponding page of the companion workbook. Download your copy at WorkLessEarnMoreBook.com.</u>

Write down your 3-5 top agency growth tactic choices:

1.

2.

3.

4.

5.

Which decision-making shortcut (logic-driven, feelings-driven, or benchmark-driven) is aligned with how *you* like to approach decisions? (If feelings-driven, re-order the list above to match how you feel now.)

Based on your preferred shortcut, narrow your list to 1-2 options that make sense for your agency:

1.

2.

Reminder: If your primary choice is particularly complicated for your agency to implement, it's okay to choose just one tactic (instead of two).

What Next?

Now that you've made some decisions, **go back to Chapter 7 and read more about your top two tactics.** (You can also find information on my blog at SakasAndCompany.com.)

At this point, it's important you commit to those one or two tactics. Why? In the next chapter, you'll draft what we've been building up to throughout this book: creating your 90-day "Work Less, Earn More" implementation plan.

Remember: **these tactics aren't forever—you're just committing to prioritize them for 90 days**. After that, you can decide whether you want (or need) to *continue* working on them. Or you may be ready to move on to different tactics to help you go from mandatory (Stage 1) or necessary (Stage 2) to needed (Stage 3)... and eventually, if you choose, to optional (Stage 4).

TL; DR
Chapter 8: Choose Your Growth Strategy
In a hurry? Here's what to know:

- In this chapter, we narrow the shortlist of 3-5 tactics to your top two, to improve your odds of success. Those two (one primary, one secondary) will be the strategy behind your 90-day plan.
- I've identified three decision-making shortcuts for agency owners: logic-driven, feelings-driven, and benchmark-driven. Make a decision using the one that seems like the best fit for you.
- Some tactics are high impact, some are quick wins, and some are both! Pick the combo you like.
- If your primary choice is particularly complicated for your agency to implement, it's okay to choose just one tactic (instead of two).
- Once you've made some decisions, go back to Chapter 7 and read more about the tactics you chose. You can find additional information on the blog at SakasAndCompany.com.
- Access all the tools and exercises mentioned here in the free companion workbook. You can download it at **WorkLessEarnMoreBook.com**.

Chapter 9:

Create Your Custom 90-Day Plan

Turning Your Vision into Reality

As an agency owner, you want to turn your ideas into action—but that's hard to do without a plan. As I learned in agency operations, **great strategies don't work without implementation.**

In this chapter, I'll walk through how to turn a strategy into a step-by-step implementation plan. I'll also share my 90-day plan template, specific to your "Work Less, Earn More" goals.

Why a 90-day plan? It's a bite-size period of time: long enough to make progress, but not so long that it feels like an eternity.

Let's look at how to create an implementation plan (in general), and then look at the 90-day plan template.

10 Steps to Create and Launch an Implementation Plan

In my coaching work, I help agency owners create custom strategies to reach their goals—and build concrete implementation plans to help them turn their new strategy into reality. The list below isn't specific to your 90-day plan—it could apply in most strategy-to-implementation situations—but think about ways it will apply.

Here's my 10-step process:

1. **Start with a strategy first:** As Stephen Covey said, "Begin with the end in mind." Once you know the right direction, you can work backwards to get there.

2. **Define your long-, medium-, and short-term key performance indicators (KPIs):** This helps you turn long-term goals into bite-size, shorter-term goals. For example, you might want to increase your agency's revenue 3X over five years. You won't get there *immediately*—but you might set a goal to grow revenue 50% in the coming year to support the five-year trajectory.

3. **Convert your long-term goals into shorter-term S.M.A.R.T. goals:** This builds from step #2, while also using the S.M.A.R.T. goals framework we discussed in Chapter 4. You'll break the big pieces into smaller pieces that can be readily assigned out to people on your team. Delegation helps you reach your goals faster and get more off of your plate as an agency owner... *if* you do it right.

4. **Organize key decisions using my values, goals, and resources (VGR) framework:** To recap from chapter 2, determine where you want to go (Goals); your motivation for getting there (Values); and the time, money, and people who'll support the process (Resources). By reducing decision fatigue, the VGR concept also applies as you manage your team, advise your clients, and make big (and not-so-big) decisions about your agency's future.

5. **Choose a project manager (PM) to lead the implementation plan:** It's hard to project-manage your own implementation plan—and that's especially true when you're an agency owner implementing your business strategy. In the next chapter, I'll share how to pick the *right* PM for your 90-day plan.

6. **Consider the change-management implications, including how each major stakeholder might react:** Most employees don't love change (at least initially), even if the changes will ultimately benefit them. But it helps to understand their *likely* reaction. Is someone likely to be supportive or opposed to the change? How does this impact your rollout plan? Change management can be a delicate thing, especially when you try to improve things too quickly.

7. **Get feedback on your implementation plan before launching it:** You'll want to stress-test the implementation plan before you make it official. Your team and your advisors will surely think of things you missed—which is an invaluable asset as you move forward. Better to catch any potential problems *before* you start the roll-out. For your 90-day plan, you may not need feedback from your entire team, but I'd at least discuss it with your leadership team and your plan's PM.

8. **Secure buy-in from your leadership team before your roll-out:** This is a natural step after getting their feedback—and it's critical to do this before you publicly announce the implementation plan to the entire agency. Because your executive managers are your day-to-day ambassadors and will be making the plan change(s) happen, you want them supporting (rather than undermining) the changes. Getting buy-in from them first can save you from a host of problems later.

9. **Be realistic about the implementation timeline... because everything takes longer than you expect:** Most things in life take longer than planned, so be realistic and build this in from the start. For example, in my work, a 3-5 point strategy might produce a list of 20-40+ implementation steps, which might take 6-12+ months to implement. Be realistic about your timeline— what can you do in 90 days? What might you need to defer?

10. **Balance quick wins vs. long-term progress:** Typically, high-impact changes take time to implement. While you're working on those, I recommend finding quick wins that you can complete easily and early. This hybrid approach helps you keep up the momentum as you work toward longer-term goals.

This method isn't *just* for large-scale agency strategy—**you can make any idea actionable by creating an implementation plan.** Perhaps even a... 90-day "Work Less, Earn More" implementation plan.

Consider agency leader **Mike Belasco**, who founded **Inflow**. Through our initial work together, I uncovered two areas to improve at his eCommerce agency: team culture and account management.

We dug deeper. According to my anonymous Culture Survey, Inflow's employees were positive about the agency's future... but less clear about their own future at the company. To fix this retention and morale challenge, I recommended creating clear career paths—so that employees could see *how* they fit into the agency's future.

Now, new team members at Inflow have a 30/60/90-day plan. And for ongoing initiatives, Mike sets company-level goals and then his team uses an Agile process to break things into chunks. Implementing these plans has helped boost team morale and work satisfaction—which in turn has led to increased employee retention. In five years, retention grew 24%.

Big ideas are great, but if your team doesn't have a clear picture of how you'll get there—and what their roles are—you'll end up with a frustrated team. And frustrated employees tend to quit.

Now that you understand *why* an implementation plan is important *and* you've got the steps to create one, let's start building your custom 90-day plan.

SHORTCUT: Use My 90-Day Plan Template to Start Working Less and Earning More

At this point, you've envisioned where you want to be, identified some short-, medium-, and long-term goals to get you there, and learned new growth strategies and tactics to help reach those goals. That means **you've got everything you need to put together your 90-day implementation plan.**

The template in the next exercise will help you create your draft plan so you can take action. This doesn't have to be perfect—it just needs to exist. Get all of your thoughts down now; you can tweak it in later revisions and throughout the feedback process.

EXERCISE: Reflect on the following questions. Record your answers here, in a doc on your computer or phone, or in the corresponding page of the companion workbook. (Tip: Need extra help filling this out? See the corresponding page of the companion workbook for a pre-filled sample template.) Download your copy at WorkLessEarnMoreBook.com.

Fill in your details to draft your 90-day implementation plan! Start by considering your long-term goal, and 1-3 annual goals to get you there.

Owner of the plan *[Your Name]*:

Project manager of the plan *[Your head of ops, a senior PM, your executive assistant, or your virtual assistant]*:

Long-term goal:

Annual goals:

- Your agency revenue goal this year:

- Your personal income goal this year:

- Any other goals for this year:

Then, add the two tactics you chose in the last chapter. This unique pairing is the high-level strategy behind your 90-day plan.

Primary tactic:

Secondary tactic (if applicable):

Now, translate each annual goal into smaller chunks (90-day, 30-day, 1-week, and right now). Start by re-confirming how the specific tactic will contribute to your annual goals.

For your primary tactic:

- **How will this support you in reaching your annual goals?**

- **90-day goal** *(What must happen in the next 90 days to make progress?)*

- **30-day goal** *(What must happen in the next 30 days to make progress?)*

- **1-week goal** *(What must happen in the next week to make progress?)*

- **Right now ("pre-goal")** *(What must happen right now? For example, as your pre-goal, you might reserve time on your calendar to complete your 1-week goal, and time for weekly reviews with your PM to keep things on track.)*

For your secondary tactic:

- **How will this support you in reaching your annual goals?**

- **90-day goal** *(What must happen in the next 90 days to make progress?)*

- **30-day goal** *(What must happen in the next 30 days to make progress?)*

- **1-week goal** *(What must happen in the next week to make progress?)*

- **Right now ("pre-goal")** *(What must happen right now?)*

Any other major goals (optional):

- **How will these support you in reaching your annual goals?**

- **90-day goal** *(What must happen in the next 90 days to make progress?)*

- **30-day goal** *(What must happen in the next 30 days to make progress?)*

- **1-week goal** *(What must happen in the next week to make progress?)*

- **Right now ("pre-goal")** *(What must happen right now?)*

Next Steps: Refine Your 90-Day Plan

Now that you've got all of your thoughts down on paper, it's time to edit and finalize your plan.

This step can't happen without feedback—so if you haven't yet identified your plan's project manager, now's the time.

If you're feeling stuck on which person to pick, you're in luck—the next chapter will help you find the right PM to keep you on track!

TL; DR
Chapter 9: Create Your Custom 90-Day Plan
In a hurry? Here's what to know:

♦ Great strategies require effective implementation, to move from ideas to action. I've developed a 10-step process that guides agency owners through what it takes to implement their strategies:
   1. Decide on a strategy, then work backwards.
   2. Define your long-, medium-, and short-term key performance indicators (KPIs).
   3. Convert your long-term goals into shorter-term S.M.A.R.T. goals, and assign them out to your team.
   4. Organize key decisions using my VGR framework.
   5. Choose a project manager to lead the implementation plan—the next chapter will help you decide who that should be, if you haven't yet.
   6. Consider the change-management implications, including how each major stakeholder might react.
   7. Get feedback on your implementation plan before launching it. For your 90-day plan, I'd at least discuss it with your plan's PM.
   8. Secure buy-in from your leadership team before your roll-out.
   9. Be realistic about the implementation timeline—because everything takes longer than you expect.
   10. Balance quick wins vs. long-term progress to help you keep up the momentum.
♦ Now you've got everything you need to put together your 90-day implementation plan—use the template in this chapter to get all of your ideas down and get started!
♦ Access all of the tools and exercises mentioned here in the free companion workbook. You can download it at **WorkLessEarnMoreBook.com.**

Chapter 10:
Hold Yourself Accountable

Start by Recruiting a Project Manager

Putting your plan into action will require support from various people—most importantly, a project manager to help you stay on track. As a former agency PM, I firmly believe that we can't project-manage our own work. You're too close to the situation.

That's why I recommend enlisting a team member to be your project manager. The right person may or may not have a formal PM title.

Consider, for example, **Nextiny** CEO **Gabriel Marguglio**. His agency had grown to become a HubSpot Diamond Solutions Partner, and he wanted customized help implementing changes to avoid a plateau in growth. When I announced my inaugural "Work Less, Earn More" bootcamp, Gabriel knew it would help him to continue his growth as an agency leader. He applied, and he got a spot!

During the bootcamp Q&A, I helped Gabriel identify some quick wins to meet his goals, but he wanted even more personalized advice. He asked to work with me one-on-one, and I developed a custom consulting project to build forward momentum and stay accountable on reaching his goals.

I identified higher-impact opportunities for Nextiny, with a priority on raising prices—especially for legacy clients who had long been paying outdated prices. I guided Gabriel through the custom strategy and implementation process, including helping him coach his customer success team on sharing the price increases with the agency's clients. Nextiny successfully landed new clients at the new higher prices and raised rates for current clients.

The initial result: Nextiny saw their best year in nearly two decades. And—after that record-breaking year—the agency generated as much revenue growth in a single *quarter* as they had in the previous year. Gabriel later reflected that the growth continued to accelerate—to the point where they've grown not only their revenue, but also their overall well-being.

Want results like that? It all comes down to accountability—bringing someone on board to help you build your plan, refine it as things change, identify obstacles *before* they happen, and keep all the pieces moving forward.

Ready to find someone to keep *you* accountable, on your way to working less and earning more? Let's look at what you should be looking for in a PM, and then decide who'll fill that role to support you in completing your 90-day plan.

It's likely your 90-day plan PM will be your assistant (if you have one) or someone from your operations team (your official #2, an operation manager, or a project manager). You already trust these team members, they're plugged into what's going on, and they're thinking about making your life easier—all of which makes them obvious choices for your 90-day plan PM.

But what if you *don't* already have someone on standby? Read on!

Seven Key Qualities for a Great PM

If you don't have someone who immediately jumps to mind, the decision is less obvious. However, the right person will *likely* have most or all of these seven key qualities:

1. **Detail-oriented:** They are good at juggling all the details involved in an implementation plan—both the planned details and the unplanned details. Get their feedback before you finalize your plan; they'll likely identify things you didn't notice.

2. **Conscientious:** If they say they'll do it, you know it'll happen. One of my clients calls them "send and delete" team members— he can send the request and delete the email, because it'll get done... and done well.

3. **Smart:** They might not be *creating* the strategy, but they need to understand how it all fits together. And they have good judgment to make decisions without having to ask you every time.

4. **Resourceful:** They're good at handling issues that pop up along the way—often solving them before you need to get involved, or at least identifying solutions so you can choose from a curated list.

5. **Trustworthy:** You're going to be telling them a lot about what's going on in your business—warts and all. You need to trust that they won't tell people who shouldn't know... *and* that they'll tell people who should.

6. **Proactive:** They take the lead in preparing, following up on, and organizing things before it's too late. They're reminding *you*, not the other way around.

7. **Intelligently disobedient:** Service dogs are trained to ignore their owner's commands if compliance would be unsafe. Likewise, your PM will (diplomatically) push back if you request something that's contrary to your goals.

Now consider: **Is there someone on your team today who:**

A. Balances your work style (e.g., they're a finisher to your starter),

B. Fits all or most of those 7 qualities,

C. *Wants* to help you,

D. And has the bandwidth to do so?

If so, congrats! You've found the project manager for your 90-day Work Less, Earn More implementation plan.

But... what if you still don't have anyone to help?

If you don't have an executive assistant or anyone else on your team who can fit this role, consider hiring a virtual assistant to support you on your 90-day plan (and to support you in general).

Keep in mind that this person can help with a wide range of things—not just your first (or future) 90-day plan.

At a high level, you have two options for hiring a VA:

A. Hire a freelance VA directly.

B. Hire someone via a VA service.

While there are pros and cons to each, I *personally* prefer direct-hire. It's more cost-effective (I tend to increase everyone's hours over time, and eventually hire some as employees when I can), I'm building a 1:1 relationship, and I see hiring people as a core part of my job.

If you aren't sure you want or need a VA, hiring via a service might make more sense—hiring is more turnkey (because the service has pre-vetted people) and they'll typically find a replacement if someone isn't a match.

Delegating to a Project Manager

So, you've selected a PM to help you implement your 90-day plan... now what? First up, you'll want to onboard them. That means getting on the same page about what you're trying to accomplish and *how* you'll work together.

Here are some tips on delegating this work so you're ready start implementing your plan:

◊ **Hold a kickoff meeting.** Start by sharing key information with your PM that will help them keep you on track, such as how you define success and how much time you'll be committing to working on your plan each week. You'll also want to use the kickoff meeting as a place to review the plan you've drafted and define roles, using the A.R.C.I. matrix (see Chapter 6).

◊ **Share your VGR.** You want your PM to know how they should operate when making decisions in a way that aligns with your VGR. This will help them get more done without having to consult you every time a question comes up. More on this in Chapter 2.

◊ **Decide: What can you delegate?** Sort out if there are things that only *you* can do as the agency leader. Ideally, you'll follow the 10-80-10 rule: You're involved in the first 10% of a project (briefing people, setting goals, etc.), your team does the 80% in the middle (implementing tactics), and you're involved in the last 10% (wrap-up). You may need to be more involved up front (and mid-way) the first time someone does something. Rather than 10/80/10, I recommend something like this: 20/30/10/40/10.

◊ **Establish a check-in cadence with your PM.** Even though you're ideally following the 10-80-10 structure, you can't check out while your team handles things. You're still actively participating in the process, not just delegating the *entire* plan to the PM. Consider how you'll continue communicating—for example, you might make this a topic in your daily scrum. I recommend checking in *at least* once a week.

Now Finalize Your Plan... And Put it Into Action!

The next step is gathering input from your team and advisors so you can finish refining your 90-day "Work Less, Earn More" implementation plan. They'll likely catch things you've missed, and team members who are closer to the front lines may have ideas around streamlining your tactics to make them easier to implement.

Once you've gathered their input, make any final revisions to your plan and commit to a "final enough" version. Note that pieces of it might change as things progress—that's okay! It doesn't have to be perfect, just good enough for now. And then... you're ready to put your plan into action!

TL; DR
Chapter 10: Hold Yourself Accountable
In a hurry? Here's what to know:

- Your team is there to support you as you implement your plans—I recommend enlisting one as your 90-day plan's project manager.
- The right person may or may not have a formal PM title. It's likely your 90-day plan PM will be your assistant or someone from your operations team.
- If you don't already have someone on standby, there are seven key qualities to look for in who to recruit—the ideal person will have all (or at least most) of these: detail-oriented, conscientious, smart, resourceful, trustworthy, proactive, and intelligently disobedient.
- If you don't have an executive assistant or anyone else on your team who can fit this role, I recommend hiring a virtual assistant to support you on your 90-day plan (and to support you in general).
- Once you've selected a PM, start by onboarding them. This includes holding a kickoff meeting; sharing your values, goals, and resources; deciding what you can delegate; and establishing a check-in cadence with your PM.
- Now... you're ready to put your plan into action!
- Access all of the tools and exercises mentioned here in the free companion workbook. You can download it at **WorkLessEarnMoreBook.com**.

Work Less, Earn More

Chapter 11:
Take Action

Launching Your Very Own Work Less, Earn More Plan

You've made it to the end of the book! You may be feeling hopeful, overwhelmed, or a mixture of both. That's totally normal.

You're embarking on an important journey. I suggest you take at least a few days before you start implementing your 90-day plan. Some of my clients like to take a short vacation to reset things.

For now, ask your PM to pre-schedule a kickoff call with you, to take place in a week or two. This will give you time to recharge and digest— and your PM can start organizing what needs to happen to put the plan into action.

Celebrate Your Progress

Before you take that short break, let's reflect on everything you've accomplished already. To recap, you have:

1. Clarified where you'd like to be in the future, by writing an Advance Retrospective to help you enlist others in getting there;

2. Designed your ideal agency, based on your unique values, goals, and resources;

3. Determined your current levels of day-to-day involvement in your agency, and set goals for your ideal involvement;

4. Grown your agency-side and personal support teams;

5. Set goals around what "work less" and "earn more" mean for you, both short- and long-term;

6. Enlisted your team to support your goals, while ideally also highlighting ways that this helps them reach *their* goals;

7. Determined where your revenue currently falls among industry benchmarks, and where it needs to be;

8. Chosen a combination of one or two growth tactics, as your priorities in the next 90 days;

9. Recruited a project manager to help you stay on track; and

10. Created your first 90-day work less, earn more plan.

This is no small feat—congrats on making it this far! You are ahead of many agency owners—in getting clear on your goals and in creating an intentional plan to reach them. That's worth celebrating.

During your pause, consider re-reading your advance retrospective vision—and make any edits that come to mind. This document will help you stay inspired as you move forward.

Remember: *Work Less, Earn More* isn't an instant fix or a single destination. You'll likely see some quick wins right away, but this is a long-term game. Be patient through the process, and celebrate your progress *and* your effort.

Start Implementing Your Plan, With Support from Your PM

As I mentioned in Chapter 6, it's often difficult for agency owners to delegate—especially when it means managing how you spend your time.

At a workshop several years ago, an agency owner bristled at my suggestion that owners enlist an employee or contractor to help them stay accountable. They said: "*I'm* the boss. *I'm* in charge. My employees don't get to tell *me* what to do." This approach *might* have worked for them... but I can't imagine it contributed to strong employee retention.

In my experience as a coach, a dictatorial mindset is short-sighted. Yes, you're the boss. But your employees *know* that. You've hired the people on your team because you value their experience and intelligence. And if they don't *like* working for you, they have options.

My advice? Embrace having the extra help. Your team can keep you accountable, and also to offer insights to make your plan run even more smoothly. They're there to help you, so *let* them.

Getting external support

Consider agency owner **Laurie Heard**. Laurie had big goals for her agency, **Move Digital**: hire great people to accomplish great things with minimal oversight and give her the ability to work remotely. This would allow her and her husband to travel more often.

Seeking guidance on where to start, Laurie reached out to me for advice. Over a few months, we built a plan around leveling-up her leadership to level-up her agency. That meant delegating sales, increasing her team's day-to-day management capabilities, and recognizing that this shift would remove Laurie as a bottleneck.

Hiring an external coach allowed Laurie to get an objective point of view on what needed to happen to reach her goals—and create accountability in the process. And then she used her in-house team to support her on a day-to-day basis, as she implemented the plan.

The result? Laurie has time to travel extensively with the confidence that her agency is in trusted hands while she's away.

This is why I urge you to not only enlist help, but to actively embrace it, whether you get implementation support internally, externally, or both.

This will help you to focus on what matters—those $1,000/hour activities that help you work less and earn more.

Staying Motivated, 90 Days at a Time

You may hit snags along the way, or you might realize that you won't be able to accomplish what you thought you would in 90 days. In those cases, I'd urge you to regroup and reframe your strategies instead of giving up. What *can* you accomplish?

Remember: Your plan doesn't need to be perfect; it just has to be good enough to get you started. Progress, not perfection.

There *is* one exception to this: If you experience a radical life change, it might make sense to hit pause and decide *how* and *when* to start again. But otherwise, stick with the 90-day plan to feel the sense of accomplishment of *finally* getting things done, even if only partially.

This 90-day plan isn't just for your agency—it's for you. Putting it into action will help you make time for yourself.

In a sense, your plan is giving you an excuse to put yourself first, when you so often put everyone else first. You're worth it!

Continuing Your Progress

Few people in the world are bold enough to run an agency. To paraphrase from former U.S. president Theodore Roosevelt, you are "the (person) in the arena."

> *"It is not the critic who counts; not the man who points out how the strong man stumbles, or where the doer of deeds could have done them better. The credit belongs to the man who is actually in the arena, whose face is marred by dust and sweat and blood; who strives valiantly; who errs, who comes short again and again, because there is no effort without error and shortcoming; but who does actually strive to do the deeds; who knows great enthusiasms, the great devotions; who spends himself in a worthy cause; who at the best knows in the end the triumph of high achievement, and who at the worst, if he fails, at least fails while daring greatly, so that his place shall never be with those cold and timid souls who neither know victory nor defeat."* –Theodore Roosevelt (1910)

It's easy for others to criticize... but you're the one *doing* it. And the steps in this book—along with your prior experience and your current and future team—will help you make things easier.

Create and implement your first 90-day "Work Less, Earn More" plan, debrief on what you learned, and repeat. It's worth the learning curve and time spent. And I know that *you can do it*—you just need to take that first step.

You've got this. If you need more advice, there's a wealth of free resources at my website (SakasAndCompany.com) and the book website (WorkLessEarnMoreBook.com). And if you get stuck, reach out for help.

Either way, I'd love to hear how it all goes. You can reach me and my team at Concierge@SakasAndCompany.com.

TL; DR
Chapter 11: Take Action

In a hurry? Here's what to know:

- Pause to celebrate what you've accomplished so far, instead of immediately jumping into implementation.
- Pre-schedule a kickoff with the person serving as PM on your 90-day plan, so they can start planning.
- Do your best to stick with the original plan, but it's okay to adjust if the situation changes significantly.
- You can always change your goals in the *next* 90-day plan. Progress, not perfection.
- Feeling stuck? Read Theodore Roosevelt's "The Man in the Arena" speech (on the previous page). It's short, and just the thing to inspire you to keep going.
- As a time-saver, download the book's companion workbook to organize and jumpstart your progress. Download it from **WorkLessEarnMore.com**

Did you start by skimming the book? Schedule time to go back and read the full book—or at least the sections that stood out the most. And consider buying an extra copy of *Work Less, Earn More* for the person serving as project manager for your 90-day plan, to help them help you.

Thanks, and good luck! –**Karl Sakas**, Sakas & Company

Additional Reading

There's always more to read! Here are books that may help (each in various ways) during your "Work Less, Earn More" journey.

Anything You Want (Derek Sivers)

Beyond Belief (John Grinnell)

The Business of Expertise (David C. Baker)

Built to Sell (John Warrillow)

Crossing the Tracks for Love (Ruby K. Payne)

Crucial Conversations (Grenny, McMillan, Switzler, Patterson)

Don't Let the Funny Stuff Get Away (Jeanne Robertson)

The Effective Manager (Mark Horstman)

The E-Myth Revisited (Michael E. Gerber)

Financial Management of a Marketing Firm (David C. Baker)

The Five Dysfunctions of a Team (Patrick Lencioni)

Founders at Work (Jessica Livingston)

The Goal (Eliyahu M. Goldratt)

How to Win Friends and Influence People (Dale Carnegie)

The Leader Lab (Tania Luna and LeeAnn Renninger)

Lost and Founder (Rand Fishkin)

Made to Lead (Karl Sakas)

Managing Humans (Michael Lopp)

Meltdown (Chris Clearfield and András Tilcsik)

The Millionaire Next Door (T.J. Stanley and W.D. Danko)

Overcoming Underearning (Barbara Stanny)

Pricing Creativity (Blair Enns)

Profit First (Mike Michalowicz)

Radical Candor (Kim Scott)

The Thought Leaders Practice (M. Church, P. Cook, S. Stein)

Traction (Gino Wickman)

Trip of a Lifetime (Paul Grescoe)

Turn the Ship Around (L. David Marquet)

When I Stop Talking, You'll Know I'm Dead (Jerry Weintraub)

Also by Karl Sakas

Hundreds of articles since 2013 at SakasAndCompany.com

The In-Demand Marketing Agency:
How to Use Public Speaking to Become an Agency of Choice (2015)

Made to Lead:
A Pocket Guide to Managing Marketing & Creative Firms (2016)

"Work Less, Earn More" Agency Growth Bootcamp
(2020 to present)

Agency Leadership Intensive (2022 to present)

Agency Lounge (2022 to present)

Acknowledgements

It's my name on the cover, but this book is very much a team effort. Specifically, thank you to:

- **Carl Smith** for writing the foreword
- **Chrissy Stalions** for the interior graphics and more
- **Diane Stadlen** as a sounding board on this and more
- **Jen Becker** for intellectual property guidance
- **Jenna Routenberg** as proofreader
- **Kate St. Cyr** as project manager and sounding board
- **Kevin Seifert** for the author photo
- **Matt Curtis** for the cover design
- **Melissa Breau** as marketing strategist
- **Nicole Capó Martínez** as editor, strategist, and more
- **Noémi Zillmann** for eBook conversion
- **Paul Panfalone** for the chapter illustrations
- **Steve Lowell** for introducing the "fuel gauge" concept

Thanks to everyone who has participated in my annual "Work Less, Earn More" bootcamps. Your feedback helped shape the advice here.

For accountability, moral support and beyond, thanks to:

- **Alexandra Watkins**
- **Amy Pirozzolo**
- **Anna Fagergren**
- **Barbara Blythe**
- **Carolyn Barry**
- **Charli Renken**
- **Daniel Orozco**
- **Elizabeth Konrath**
- **Evan Carroll**
- **Fred Acurero**
- **Joanna Sandford**
- **Katie Connors**
- **Kat Spasov**
- **Kris Jecen**

- ♥ **Laura Richards**
- ♥ **Laura Westman**
- ♥ **Michael Hobgood**
- ♥ **Nick Zimmerman**
- ♥ **Rachel Andrea Go**
- ♥ **Stan Phelps**
- ♥ **Steph Brontman**
- ♥ **Tyler Holt**

A special thanks to clients who agreed to my sharing their case studies:

- ♥ **Chris Dreyer** (Rankings.io)
- ♥ **Chris Heiler** (Landscape Leadership)
- ♥ **Dale Bertrand** (Fire&Spark)
- ♥ **Gabriel Marguglio** (Nextiny)
- ♥ **Joe Quinn** (Big Vision)
- ♥ **Julie Thorner** (Liquid Spark)
- ♥ **Laurie Heard** (Move Digital)
- ♥ **Mike Belasco** (Inflow)
- ♥ **Mike King** (iPullRank)
- ♥ **Nicolas Jacobeus** (Belighted)
- ♥ **Rhoan Morgan** (DemandLab)

Thanks to everyone who shared an "advance review" blurb:

- ♥ **Blair Enns**
- ♥ **Brent Weaver**
- ♥ **Cathy Atkins**
- ♥ **Chris Dreyer**
- ♥ **David C. Baker**
- ♥ **Drew McLellan**
- ♥ **Erin Bury**
- ♥ **Gini Dietrich**
- ♥ **Gray MacKenzie**
- ♥ **Jay Baer**
- ♥ **Neen James**
- ♥ **Steve Krull**
- ♥ **Tamsen Webster**
- ♥ **Tara Coomans**

Thanks to teachers, mentors, managers, and early-career clients, including:

- ♥ Alan Wishengrad
- ♥ Andrea Nemeth
- ♥ Angela Williams
- ♥ Beth Pretty
- ♥ Bettie Stegall
- ♥ Celine Suarez
- ♥ Chad Smith
- ♥ Christopher Bonner
- ♥ George Smart
- ♥ Heather Hesketh
- ♥ Herrington Bryce
- ♥ Jake St. Peter
- ♥ Jason Stanley
- ♥ Jeff MacDonagh
- ♥ Jerre Johnson
- ♥ Jerry Berenty
- ♥ Jim Whittenburg
- ♥ Joyce Stern
- ♥ Julie Agnew
- ♥ Ken Nostro
- ♥ Kelly Shaver
- ♥ Kimberly Gladman
- ♥ Kyle Johnson
- ♥ Lisa Greeves
- ♥ Lisa Szykman
- ♥ Mary Catherine Bunde
- ♥ Mike Dickerson
- ♥ Mike Hanbridge
- ♥ Paul Renard
- ♥ Sally Haynes
- ♥ Steve Champeon
- ♥ Thomas Ingham

And thanks to family and friends for your support—including advice from my parents on business and leadership.

About the Author

Running an agency is complex, but it doesn't have to be so complicated. **Karl Sakas** helps agency leaders make smarter decisions for smoother growth.

Karl is a fourth-generation business owner with decades of consulting experience. As a management consultant and executive coach, Karl has personally advised hundreds of agency owners on every inhabited continent.

Through Sakas & Company, Karl offers coaching, consulting, and training. Channeling his background in agency operations, his clients often call him their "agency therapist" (but he is not an actual therapist).

Karl has written three books and more than 400 articles on agency growth. Outside of work, Karl volunteers as a bartender on an antique train, mixing martinis at 100 miles an hour.

To learn more, visit SakasAndCompany.com, AgencyLounge.com, and WorkLessEarnMoreBook.com.

Made in United States
North Haven, CT
01 February 2023

31961934R00104